Blest Are Those Who Mourn

Blest Are Those Who Mourn

Music for the Order of Christian Funerals

Second Edition

GIA Publications, Inc.
Chicago

G-8577
Copyright © 2013 by GIA Publications, Inc.
7404 South Mason Avenue, Chicago, Illinois 60638
www.giamusic.com

Cover design by Martha Chlipala.

ISBN 978-1-62277-003-8

1 2 3 4 5 6 7 8 9 10 11 12 13 14 15 16 17 18 19 20

FOREWORD

In the face of death, the Church confidently proclaims that God has created each person for eternal life and that Jesus, the Son of God, by his death and resurrection, has broken the chains of sin and death that bound humanity. Christ "achieved his task of redeeming humanity and giving perfect glory to God, principally by the paschal mystery of his blessed passion, resurrection from the dead, and glorious ascension."[1]

Order of Christian Funerals, 1

First published in 1989, the Catholic Church's *Order of Christian Funerals* is held in high esteem by clergy and parish ministers. It is a comprehensive collection of liturgical rites and prayers for the deceased as well as for grieving family members and friends. In addition to the funeral Mass, the *Order of Christian Funerals* provides rites and prayers for those most private (and frequently most difficult) moments that a family encounters at the death of a loved one. These moments include the gathering in the presence of the deceased after death, the first viewing of the body in the coffin, the final closing of the coffin, and the final committal of the body or cremated remains to the ground or mausoleum. Parishes would do well to draw upon the wealth of rites and prayers the Church makes available. Music can be an important element of all these rites as "it allows the community to express convictions and feelings that words alone may fail to convey."[2] To that end, we are pleased to offer this selection of music for the *Order of Christian Funerals*.

Originally published in 1993, this revised edition of *Blest Are Those Who Mourn* features an expanded selection of psalmody, hymns, and songs. In order to reflect the growing diversity of the Catholic Church in the United States, a number of selections appear bilingually in English and Spanish; some songs also include additional languages. Select Latin chants have been added as well as newer compositions that were written after the publication of the original edition. In addition to a complete order of service for the funeral liturgy, outlines are included for the vigil for the deceased (wake service) and the rite of committal.

Through music, one can find both consolation and confidence. As Christians grieve the loss of a loved one, so to do they rejoice in the new life Christ now gives to the deceased. We hope that this collection of music will assist all who mourn as they sing of the resurrection promised through Christ's victory over death.

David Anderson
Michael Silhavy

---

[1] *Sacrosanctum Concilium,* 5
[2] *Order of Christian Funerals,* 30

Contents

Funeral Liturgy

The rites which surround the death of a Christian extend from Viaticum (the last Holy Communion) and final prayers before death through the wake service and funeral liturgy to the burial of the body or cremated remains. In all of this the community affirms its faith in the communion of saints and the resurrection of the dead. The family and friends are helped in their time of sorrow with prayer and song. Thus they express present grief even as they hold to the Church's lasting hope.

The funeral liturgy may be celebrated within Mass or outside Mass.

INTRODUCTORY RITES
GREETING   1
All stand as the priest (or deacon) greets the assembly at the door, using these or other words:

> *Priest:* Grace to you and peace from God our Father
> and the Lord Jesus Christ.

> *Assembly:* **And with your spirit.**

The body or cremated remains is sprinkled with holy water, a reminder of baptism. The family or pall bearers spread the pall, a garment like that which the Christian received at baptism, over the coffin.

PROCESSION   2
The funeral procession then moves into the church accompanied by the following or an appropriate hymn or psalm.

Refrain

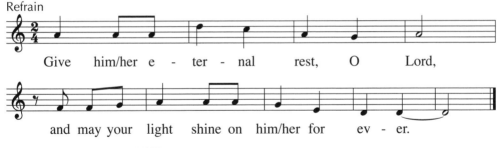

Give him/her e - ter - nal rest, O Lord, and may your light shine on him/her for ev - er.

Text: *Order of Christian Funerals*, © 1985, ICEL
Music: Robert J. Batastini, © 1986, GIA Publications, Inc.

Verses

I love the LORD, for he has heard
my voice, my appeal;
for he has turned his ear to me
whenever I call. ℟.

They surrounded me, the snares of death;
the anguish of the grave has found me;
anguish and sorrow I found.
I called on the name of the LORD:
"Deliver my soul, O LORD!" ℟.

How gracious is the LORD, and just;
our God has compassion.

The LORD protects the simple;
I was brought low, and he saved me. ℟.

Turn back, my soul, to your rest,
for the LORD has been good to you;
he has kept my soul from death,
my eyes from tears, and my feet from
    stumbling. ℟.

I will walk in the presence of the LORD
in the land of the living.
Praise the Father, the Son and Holy Spirit,
for ever and ever. ℟.

Text: Psalm 116A, *The Revised Grail Psalms*, © 2010, Conception Abbey and The Grail, admin. by GIA Publications, Inc.
Music: Joseph Gelineau, SJ, © 1963, The Grail, GIA Publications, Inc., agent

OPENING PRAYER

After silent prayer, the priest concludes the introductory rites with a solemn prayer, to which all respond: **Amen.** *All are then seated.*

LITURGY OF THE WORD

READINGS

One or more passages from Scripture are read. At the conclusion of each:

Reader: The word of the Lord.

Assembly: **Thanks be to God.**

3 RESPONSORIAL PSALM

The following psalm may be sung after the first reading; for additional psalms, see nos. 26–46.

Refrain

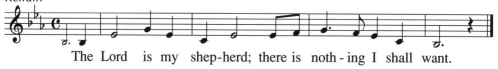

The Lord is my shep-herd; there is noth-ing I shall want.

Text: *Lectionary for Mass,* © 1969, 1981, 1997, ICEL
Music: Richard Proulx, © 1975, GIA Publications, Inc.

Verses

The LORD is my shepherd;
there is nothing I shall want.
Fresh and green are the pastures
where he gives me repose.
Near restful waters he leads me;
he revives my soul. ℟.

He guides me along the right path,
for the sake of his name.
Though I should walk in the valley
    of the shadow of death,
no evil would I fear, for you are with me.

Your crook and your staff will give
    me comfort. ℟.

You have prepared a table before me
in the sight of my foes.
My head you have anointed with oil;
my cup is overflowing. ℟.

Surely goodness and mercy shall follow
    me
all the days of my life.
In the LORD's own house shall I dwell
for length of days unending. ℟.

Text: Psalm 23, *The Revised Grail Psalms,* © 2010, Conception Abbey and The Grail, admin. by GIA Publications, Inc.

4 GOSPEL

Before the gospel reading, all stand as an acclamation is sung:

Al - le - lu - ia,   al - le - lu - ia,   al - le - lu - ia.

Music: Chant Mode VI; acc. by Richard Proulx, © 1985, GIA Publications, Inc.

During Lent:

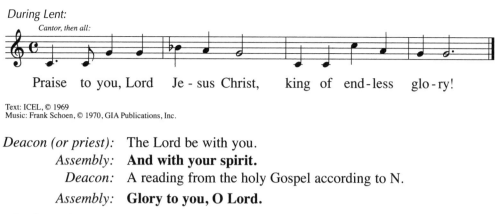

Praise to you, Lord Je - sus Christ, king of end - less glo - ry!

Text: ICEL, © 1969
Music: Frank Schoen, © 1970, GIA Publications, Inc.

Deacon (or priest): The Lord be with you.
Assembly: **And with your spirit.**
Deacon: A reading from the holy Gospel according to N.
Assembly: **Glory to you, O Lord.**

After the reading:

Deacon: The Gospel of the Lord.
Assembly: **Praise to you, Lord Jesus Christ.**

HOMILY *(All sit)*

PRAYER OF THE FAITHFUL 5
All stand and join in prayer for the deceased, for grieving family members and friends, and for the needs of the Church and the world.

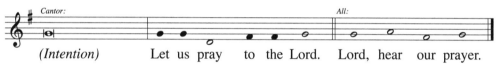

(Intention) Let us pray to the Lord. Lord, hear our prayer.

Music: Byzantine chant

When the funeral liturgy is celebrated outside Mass, the final commendation follows the prayer of the faithful.

LITURGY OF THE EUCHARIST 6
To celebrate the Eucharist means to give God thanks and praise. When the altar has been prepared with the bread and wine, the assembly joins the priest in remembering the gracious gifts of God in creation and God's saving deeds. The center of this is the paschal mystery, the death of our Lord Jesus Christ which destroyed the power of death and his rising which brings us life. That mystery into which we were baptized we proclaim each Sunday at the Eucharist. It is the very shape of Christian life.

PRESENTATION AND PREPARATION OF THE GIFTS
Bread and wine are brought to the altar and the deacon or priest prepares these gifts. If there is no music, the prayers may be said aloud, and all may respond: **Blessed be God for ever.** *The priest then invites all to pray.*

Priest: Pray, brethren (brothers and sisters),
that my sacrifice and yours
may be acceptable to God, the almighty Father.
(All stand)
Assembly: **May the Lord accept the sacrifice at your hands**
for the praise and glory of his name,
for our good and the good of all his holy Church.

7 EUCHARISTIC PRAYER

The central prayer of the Mass begins with this dialogue between priest and assembly.

> *Priest:* The Lord be with you.
> *Assembly:* **And with your spirit.**
> *Priest:* Lift up your hearts.
> *Assembly:* **We lift them up to the Lord.**
> *Priest:* Let us give thanks to the Lord our God.
> *Assembly:* **It is right and just.**

The Holy, Holy, Holy acclamation is sung to conclude the introduction to the eucharistic prayer.

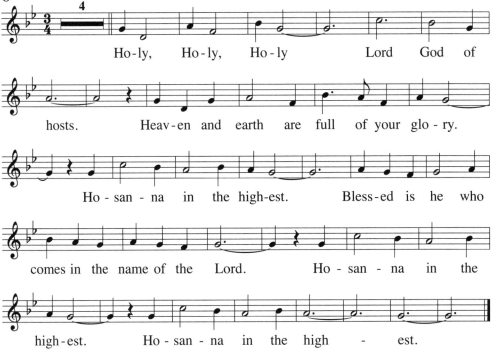

Ho-ly, Ho-ly, Ho-ly Lord God of hosts. Heav-en and earth are full of your glo-ry. Ho - san - na in the high-est. Bless-ed is he who comes in the name of the Lord. Ho - san - na in the high-est. Ho - san - na in the high - est.

Text: ICEL, © 2010
Music: *Mass of Creation,* Marty Haugen, © 1984, 1985, 2010, GIA Publications, Inc.

Or:

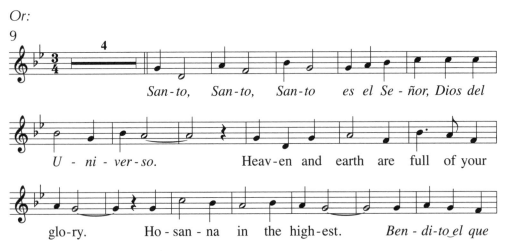

San-to, San-to, San-to es el Se - ñor, Dios del U - ni - ver - so. Heav-en and earth are full of your glo-ry. Ho - san - na in the high-est. Ben - di-to el que

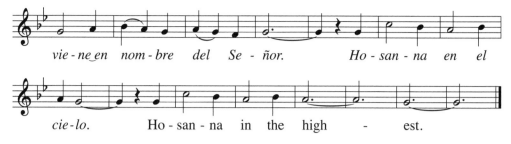

Text: English, ICEL, © 2010
Music: *Mass of Creation*, Marty Haugen; adapt. by Tony E. Alonso, © 1984, 1985, 2010, 2013, GIA Publications, Inc.

One of the following acclamations follows the priest's invitation: "The mystery of faith."

Text: ICEL, © 2010
Music: *Mass of Creation*, Marty Haugen, © 2010, GIA Publications, Inc.

Or:

Text: English, ICEL, © 2010
Music: *Mass of Creation*, Marty Haugen; adapt. by Tony E. Alonso, © 2010, 2013, GIA Publications, Inc.

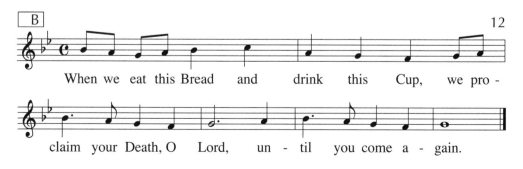

Text: ICEL, © 2010
Music: *Mass of Creation*, Marty Haugen, © 2010, GIA Publications, Inc.

Or:

13

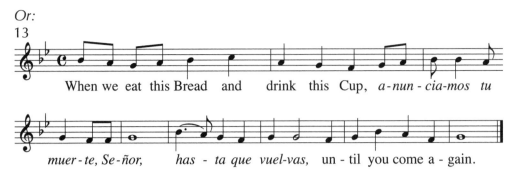

When we eat this Bread and drink this Cup, *a-nun-cia-mos tu muer-te, Se-ñor,* *has-ta que vuel-vas,* un-til you come a-gain.

Text: English, ICEL, © 2010
Music: *Mass of Creation,* Marty Haugen; adapt. by Tony E. Alonso, © 2010, 2013, GIA Publications, Inc.

14

C

Save us, Sav-ior of the world, for by your Cross and Res-ur-rec-tion you have set us free, you have set us free.

Text: ICEL, © 2010
Music: *Mass of Creation,* Marty Haugen, © 2010, GIA Publications, Inc.

Or:

15

Save us, Sav-ior of the world, *por tu cruz y re-su-rrec-ción nos has sal-va-do, Se-ñor,* you have set us free.

Text: English, ICEL, © 2010
Music: *Mass of Creation,* Marty Haugen; adapt. by Tony E. Alonso, © 2010, 2013, GIA Publications, Inc.

16 *The eucharistic prayer concludes:*

Priest: Through him, and with him, and in him,
      O God, almighty Father,
      in the unity of the Holy Spirit,
      all glory and honor is yours,
      for ever and ever.

A-men, a-men, a-men.
A-mén, a-mén, a-mén.

A - men, a - men, a - men.
A - mén, a - mén, a - mén.

Music: *Mass of Creation*, Marty Haugen; adapt. by Tony E. Alonso, © 1984, 1985, 2010, 2013, GIA Publications, Inc.

COMMUNION RITE 17

The priest invites all to join in the Lord's Prayer.

Assembly: **Our Father, who art in heaven,**
hallowed be thy name;
thy kingdom come,
thy will be done on earth as it is in heaven.
Give us this day our daily bread,
and forgive us our trespasses,
as we forgive those who trespass against us;
and lead us not into temptation,
but deliver us from evil.

Priest: Deliver us, Lord...and the coming of our Savior, Jesus Christ.

Assembly: **For the kingdom, the power, and the glory are yours**
now and for ever.

SIGN OF PEACE

Priest: Lord Jesus Christ, who said...for ever and ever.
Assembly: **Amen.**
Priest: The peace of the Lord be with you always.
Assembly: **And with your spirit.**

All exchange a sign of peace.

Then the eucharistic bread is solemnly broken and the consecrated bread and wine are prepared for Holy Communion. The litany "Lamb of God" is sung during the breaking of the bread.

18

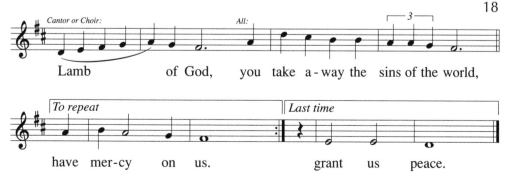

Lamb of God, you take a-way the sins of the world,

To repeat   *Last time*

have mer-cy on us.   grant us peace.

Music: *Holy Cross Mass*, David Clark Isele, © 1979, GIA Publications, Inc.

Or:

19

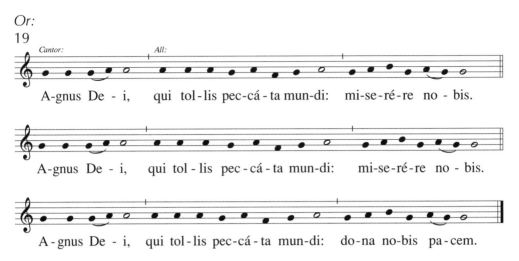

A-gnus De - i, qui tol-lis pec-cá - ta mun-di: mi-se-ré-re no - bis.

A-gnus De - i, qui tol - lis pec - cá - ta mun-di: mi-se-ré-re no - bis.

A - gnus De - i, qui tol-lis pec-cá - ta mun-di: do-na no-bis pa - cem.

Music: Vatican Edition XVIII; acc. by Robert J. Batastini, © 1993, GIA Publications, Inc.

Priest: Behold the Lamb of God,
behold him who takes away the sins of the world.
Blessed are those called to the supper of the Lamb.

Assembly: **Lord, I am not worthy that you should enter under my roof,
but only say the word and my soul shall be healed.**

Minister of communion: The Body (Blood) of Christ.
Communicant: **Amen.**

While the priest is receiving the Body of Christ, the communion song or psalm begins. After all have received communion, all stand for the prayer to which all respond: **Amen.** *If the final commendation is to be celebrated at the place of committal, the procession to the place of committal immediately follows the prayer after communion.*

20 FINAL COMMENDATION
After an invitation to prayer, all pray silently. The body or cremated remains may then be sprinkled with holy water and incensed, or this may take place during or after the song of farewell.

21 SONG OF FAREWELL
The following or another appropriate responsory (see nos. 23–25, 146 and 147) or song may be sung.

Refrain

Re - ceive his/her soul, re - ceive his/her soul,
Re - ci - ban su al - ma, re - ci - ban su al - ma,

and pre - sent him/her to God the Most High,
y pre - sén - ten - la an - te el Al - tí - si - mo,

All:

and pre - sent him/her to God the Most High.
y pre - sén - ten - la an - te el Al - tí - si - mo.

Verses

1. Saints of God, come to his/her aid!
   Hasten to meet him/her, angels of the
   Lord!

2. May Christ, who called you, take you
   to himself;
   may angels lead you to the bosom of
   Abraham.

3. Eternal rest grant unto him/her, O Lord,
   and let perpetual light shine upon
   him/her.

1. ¡Vengan en su ayuda, santos de Dios!
   ¡Salgan a su encuentro, ángeles del
   Señor!

2. Cristo, que te llamó, te reciba;
   y los ángeles te conduzcan al regazo
   de Abrahán.

3. Concédele, Señor, el descanso eterno,
   y brille para ella/él la luz perpetua.

Text: *Order of Christian Funerals,* © 1985, ICEL; *Ritual de Exequias,* © 1989, Comisión Episcopal Española de Liturgia
Tune: Steven R. Janco, b. 1961, © 1990, GIA Publications, Inc.

PRAYER OF COMMENDATION   22
At the conclusion of the prayer all respond: **Amen.**

PROCESSION TO THE PLACE OF COMMITTAL
Deacon or priest: In peace let us take our brother/sister to his/her place of rest.

SONG
As the assembly leaves the church, a song may be sung.

Music for the Final Commendation

23 SAINTS OF GOD

Cantor:

1. Saints of God, come to his/her aid!
2. May Christ who called you, take you to him-self;
3. Give him/her e - ter - nal rest, O Lord,

Come to meet him,/her, an - gels of the
may an - gels lead you to A - bra - ham's
and may your light shine on him/her for

Lord!
side. Re - ceive his/her soul and pre - sent him/her to
ev - er.

All:

God, to God the Most High. Re - ceive his/her soul

and pre - sent him/her to God, to God the Most High.

Text: *Order of Christian Funerals*; alt. by Richard Proulx
Music: Richard Proulx
© 1975, GIA Publications, Inc.

24 SAINTS OF GOD

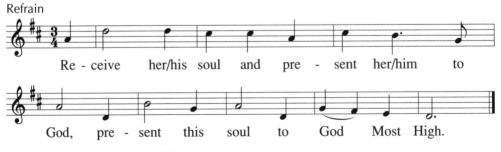

Refrain

Re - ceive her/his soul and pre - sent her/him to

God, pre - sent this soul to God Most High.

Text: *Order of Christian Funerals*; para. by David Haas
Music: David Haas
© 1990, GIA Publications, Inc.

Text: *Rite of Funerals,* © 1970, ICEL
Tune: Howard Hughes, SM, b.1930, © 1977, ICEL

Psalms

26 Psalm 23: My Shepherd Is the Lord

Antiphon I

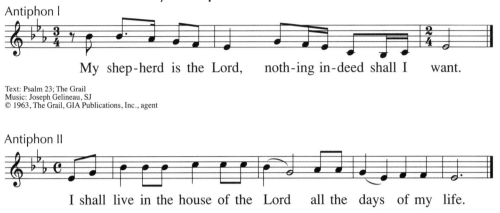

My shep-herd is the Lord, noth-ing in-deed shall I want.

Text: Psalm 23; The Grail
Music: Joseph Gelineau, SJ
© 1963, The Grail, GIA Publications, Inc., agent

Antiphon II

I shall live in the house of the Lord all the days of my life.

Text: *Lectionary for Mass,* © 1969, 1981, 1997, ICEL
Music: Robert J. Batastini, © 1975, GIA Publications, Inc.

Verses

1. The LORD is my shepherd;
   there is nothing I shall want.
   Fresh and green are the pastures
   where he gives me repose.
   Near restful waters he leads me;
   he revives my soul.

2. He guides me along the right path,
   for the sake of his name.
   Though I should walk in the valley
   of the shadow of death,
   no evil would I fear, for you are with me.
   Your crook and your staff will give me comfort.

3. You have prepared a table before me
   in the sight of my foes.
   My head you have anointed with oil;
   my cup is overflowing.

4. Surely goodness and mercy shall follow me
   all the days of my life.
   In the LORD's own house shall I dwell
   for length of days unending.

Text: Psalm 23: *The Revised Grail Psalms,* © 2010, Conception Abbey and The Grail, admin. by GIA Publications, Inc.

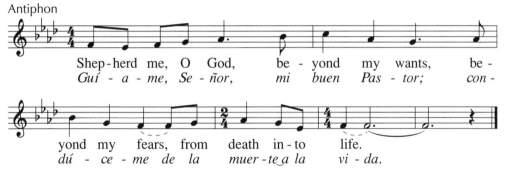

Antiphon

Shep-herd me, O God, be - yond my wants, be -
Guí - a - me, Se - ñor, mi buen Pas - tor; con -

yond my fears, from death in - to life.
dú - ce - me de la muer - te_a la vi - da.

Verses

1. God is my shepherd, so nothing shall I want;
   I rest in the meadows of faithfulness and love;
   I walk by the quiet waters of peace.

2. Gently you raise me and heal my weary soul;
   you lead me by pathways of righteousness and truth;
   my spirit shall sing the music of your name.

3. Though I should wander the valley of death, I fear no evil, for you are at my side;
   your rod and your staff, my comfort and my hope.

4. You have set me a banquet of love in the face of hatred,
   crowning me with love beyond my pow'r to hold.

5. Surely your kindness and mercy follow me all the days of my life;
   I will dwell in the house of my God forevermore.

1. *Tú_eres mi pastor, y nada me falta: en verdes praderas me haces reposar.*
   Hacia fuentes tranquilas me quieres conducir.

2. *Cuán tiernamente mi alma fortaleces; por siempre me guías por sendas de verdad;*
   se_alegra mi_espíritu en tu santo nombre.

3. *Aunque camine por cañadas oscuras, no temo nada, porque tú vas conmigo.*
   Tu vara_y tu cayado: ellos me sosiegan.

4. *Tú preparas una mesa_ante mí, enfrente de mis enemigos;*
   me_unges la cabeza, y mi copa rebosa.

5. *Me_acompañarán tu bondad y tu merced todos los días de mi vida.*
   Habitaré en la casa del Señor por años sin término.

Text: Psalm 23; Marty Haugen, b.1950; tr. by Ronald F. Krisman, b.1946
Tune: Marty Haugen, b.1950

28 Psalm 23: The Lord Is My Shepherd

Refrain

The Lord is my shep-herd; there is noth-ing I shall want.

Verses

1. The LORD is my shepherd;
   there is nothing I shall want.
   Fresh and green are the pastures
   where he gives me repose.
   Near restful waters he leads me;
   he revives my soul.

2. He guides me along the right path,
   for the sake of his name.
   Though I should walk in the valley of the shadow of death,
   no evil would I fear, for you are with me.
   Your crook and your staff will give me comfort.

3. You have prepared a table before me
   in the sight of my foes.
   My head you have anointed with oil;
   my cup is overflowing.

4. Surely goodness and mercy shall follow me
   all the days of my life.
   In the LORD's own house shall I dwell
   for length of days unending.

Text: Psalm 23: *The Revised Grail Psalms,* © 2010, Conception Abbey and The Grail, admin. by GIA Publications, Inc.; refrain, *Lectionary for Mass,*
© 1969, 1981, 1997, ICEL
Music: Michel Guimont, © 1994, GIA Publications, Inc.

Antiphon I*

The Lord is my shep-herd; there is noth-ing I shall want. The Lord is my shep-herd; noth-ing shall I fear.

Antiphon II*

El Se-ñor es mi pas-tor, na-da me fal-ta. El Se-ñor es mi pas-tor, na-da me fal-ta.

Verses

1. The LORD is my shepherd;
   there is nothing I shall want.
   Fresh and green are the pastures
   where he gives me repose.
   Near restful waters he leads me;
   he revives my soul.

2. He guides me along the right path,
   for the sake of his name.
   Though I should walk in the valley of the
      shadow of death,
   no evil would I fear, for you are with me.
   Your crook and your staff will give
      me comfort.

3. You have prepared a table before me
   in the sight of my foes.
   My head you have anointed with oil;
   my cup is overflowing.

4. Surely goodness and mercy shall
      follow me
   all the days of my life.
   In the LORD's own house shall I dwell
   for length of days unending.

1. El Señor es mi pastor, nada me falta:
   en verdes praderas me hace recostar;
   me conduce hacia fuentes tranquilas
   y repara mis fuerzas.

2. Me guía por el sendero justo,
   por el honor de su nombre.
   Aunque camine por cañadas oscuras,
   nada temo, porque tú vas conmigo:
   tu vara y tu cayado
   me sosiegan.

3. Preparas una mesa ante mí,
   enfrente de mis enemigos;
   me unges la cabeza con perfume,
   y mi copa rebosa.

4. Tu bondad y tu misericordia
      me acompañan
   todos los días de mi vida,
   y habitaré en la casa del Señor
   por años sin término.

Antiphons I and II may be sung simultaneously.

Text: Psalm 23; English antiphon, *Lectionary for Mass*, © 1969, 1981, 1997, ICEL; verses, *The Revised Grail Psalms*, © 2010, Conception Abbey and The Grail, admin. by GIA Publication, Inc.; Spanish text, *Leccionario, Edición Hispanoamérica*, © 1970, 1972, Conferencia Episcopal Española
Music: Antiphons, Ronald F. Krisman, © 2004, GIA Publications, Inc.; verses, Michel Guimont, © 1994, 1998, GIA Publications, Inc.

30　Psalm 25: To You, O Lord

Antiphon

To you, O Lord, I lift my soul.

Text: Psalm 25:1; © 1963, The Grail, GIA Publications, Inc., agent
Music: Robert J. Thompson, © 1975, GIA Publications, Inc.

Verses

1. Remember your compassion, O LORD,
   and your merciful love, for they are from of old.
   Do not remember the sins of my youth.
   In your merciful love remember me.

2. Relieve the anguish of my heart,
   and set me free from my distress.
   See my lowliness and suffering,
   and take away all my sins.

3. Preserve my life and rescue me.
   Let me not be put to shame, for in you I trust.
   May integrity and virtue protect me,
   for I have hoped in you, O LORD.

Text: Psalm 25:6–7a and c, 17, 20–21; *The Revised Grail Psalms*, © 2010, Conception Abbey and The Grail, admin. by GIA Publications, Inc.
Music: A. Gregory Murray, OSB, © L. J. Carey and Co., Ltd.

31　Psalm 25: To You, O Lord / A Ti, Señor

Antiphon*

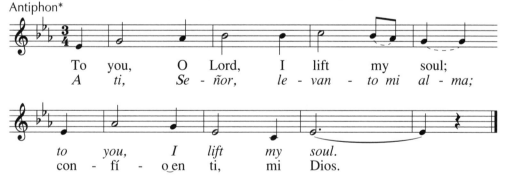

To you, O Lord, I lift my soul;
A ti, Se - ñor, le - van - to mi al - ma;

to you, I lift my soul.
con - fí - o en ti, mi Dios.

Verses

1. Lord, make me know your ways, teach me your paths
   and keep me in the way of your truth, for you are God, my Savior.

2. For the Lord is good and righteous, revealing the way to those who wander,
   gently leading the poor and the humble.

3. To the ones who seek the Lord, who look to God's word, who live God's love,
   God will always be near, and will show them mercy.

*For a bilingual antiphon, sing the text in italics.

1. *En tu verdad, Señor, guía mis pasos,*
   hazme caminar con lealtad; ven, sálvame, Dios mío.

2. *El Señor es bueno y recto, mostrando a los pecadores la senda;*
   a los pobres enseña su camino.

3. *Los que buscan al Señor, siguiendo su luz, viviendo en su amor,*
   junto a Dios estarán, y verán su clemencia.

Text: Psalm 25:4–5, 8–9, 12–14, Marty Haugen, © 1982, GIA Publications, Inc.; English antiphon, *Lectionary for Mass*, © 1969, 1981, 1997, ICEL;
Spanish tr. by Ronald F. Krisman, © 2012, GIA Publications, Inc.
Music: Marty Haugen, © 1982, GIA Publications, Inc.

Psalm 27: The Lord Is My Light / 32
Mi Luz y Salvación

Antiphon

The Lord is my light and my sal - va - tion, of
Mi luz y sal - va - ción es el Se - ñor, ¿a

whom should I be a - fraid, of whom should I be a - fraid?
quién te - me - ré, a quién te - me - ré?

Verses

1. The Lord is my light and my help; whom should I fear?
   The Lord is the stronghold of my life; before whom should I shrink?

2. There is one thing I ask of the Lord; for this I long:
   to live in the house of the Lord all the days of my life.

3. I believe I shall see the goodness of the Lord in the land of the living;
   hope in God, and take heart. Hope in the Lord!

1. *El Señor es mi luz y salvación, ¿a quién temeré?*
   El Señor es la defensa de mi vida, ¿quién me hará temblar?

2. *Le pido al Señor una cosa, eso buscaré:*
   habitar en la casa del Señor por los días de mi vida.

3. *La bondad del Señor, mi Dios, espero ver en el país de la vida;*
   confía en el Señor, espera en el Señor.

Text: Psalm 27:1–2, 4, 13–14; David Haas; tr. by Ronald F. Krisman
Music: David Haas
© 1983, tr. 2012, GIA Publications, Inc.

33 Psalm 27: The Lord Is My Light

Antiphon I

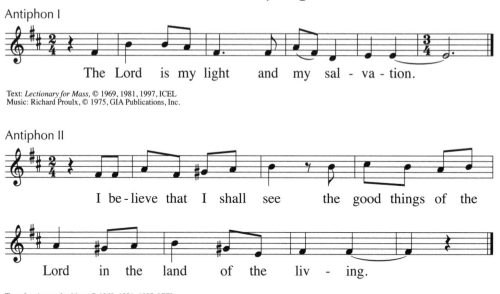

The Lord is my light and my sal - va - tion.

Text: *Lectionary for Mass,* © 1969, 1981, 1997, ICEL
Music: Richard Proulx, © 1975, GIA Publications, Inc.

Antiphon II

I be - lieve that I shall see the good things of the

Lord in the land of the liv - ing.

Text: *Lectionary for Mass,* © 1969, 1981, 1997, ICEL
Music: Columba Kelly, OSB, harm. by Richard Proulx, © 1975, GIA Publications, Inc.

Verses

1. The LORD is my light and my salvation;
   whom shall I fear?
   The LORD is the stronghold of my life;
   whom should I dread?

2. There is one thing I ask of the LORD,
   only this do I seek:
   to live in the house of the LORD
   all the days of my life,
   to gaze on the beauty of the LORD,
   to inquire at his temple.

3. O LORD, hear my voice when I call;
   have mercy and answer me.
   Of you my heart has spoken,
   "Seek his face."

4. I believe I shall see the LORD's goodness
   in the land of the living.
   Wait for the LORD; be strong;
   be stouthearted, and wait for the LORD!

Text: Psalm 27:1, 4, 7–8, 13–14; *The Revised Grail Psalms,* © 2010, Conception Abbey and The Grail, admin. by GIA Publications, Inc., agent

Antiphon I

Like a deer that longs for run - ning streams, my soul longs for you, my God.

Text: *Lectionary for Mass*, © 1969, 1981, 1997, ICEL
Music: Richard Proulx. © 1986, GIA Publications, Inc.

Antiphon II

My soul is thirst - ing for the Lord: when shall I see God face to face?

Text: Psalm 42:3, The Grail
Music: Joseph Gelineau, SJ
© 1963, 1993, The Grail, GIA Publications, Inc., agent

Verses

1. Like the deer that yearns
   for running streams,
   so my soul is yearning
   for you, my God.

2. My soul is thirsting for God,
   the living God;
   when can I enter and appear
   before the face of God?

3. O send forth your light and your truth;
   they will guide me on.
   They will bring me to your holy mountain,
   to the place where you dwell.

4. And I will come to the altar of God,
   to God, my joy and gladness.
   To you will I give thanks on the harp,
   O God, my God.

5. Why are you cast down, my soul;
   why groan within me?
   Hope in God; I will praise him yet again,
   my saving presence and my God.

Text: Psalm 42:2, 3; Psalm 43:3, 4, 5; *The Revised Grail Psalms*, © 2010, Conception Abbey and The Grail, admin. by GIA Publications, Inc., agent

35 Psalm 62: Rest in God Alone

Antiphon

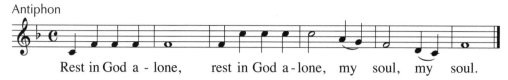

Rest in God a - lone, rest in God a - lone, my soul, my soul.

Text: *Lectionary for Mass*, © 1969, 1981, 1997, ICEL
Music: Robert J. Batastini, © 1975, GIA Publications, Inc.

Verses

1. In God alone is my soul at rest;
   my salvation comes from him.
   He alone is my rock, my salvation,
   my fortress; never shall I falter.

2. In God alone be at rest, my soul,
   for my hope is from him.
   He alone is my rock, my salvation,
   my fortress; never shall I falter.

3. In God is my salvation and glory,
   my rock of strength;
   in God is my refuge.
   Trust him at all times, O people.
   Pour out your hearts before him.

Text: Psalm 62:2–3, 6–7, 8–9ab; *The Revised Grail Psalms*, © 2010, Conception Abbey and The Grail, admin. by GIA Publications, Inc., agent

Antiphon

My soul is thirst-ing for you, O Lord, thirst-ing for you my God.

Text: *Lectionary for Mass,* © 1969, 1981, 1997, ICEL
Music: Richard Proulx, © 1975, GIA Publications, Inc.

Verses

1. O God, you are my God; at dawn I seek you;
   for you my soul is thirsting.
   For you my flesh is pining,
   like a dry, weary land without water.

2. I have come before you in the sanctuary,
   to behold your strength and your glory.
   Your loving mercy is better than life;
   my lips will speak your praise.

3. I will bless you all my life;
   in your name I will lift up my hands.
   My soul shall be filled as with a banquet;
   with joyful lips, my mouth shall praise you.

4. For you have been my strength;
   in the shadow of your wings I rejoice.
   My soul clings fast to you;
   your right hand upholds me.

Text: Psalm 63:2, 3–4, 5–6, 8–9; *The Revised Grail Psalms,* © 2010, Conception Abbey and The Grail, admin. by GIA Publications, Inc.

37 Psalm 91: Be with Me, Lord / Acompáñame

Antiphon*

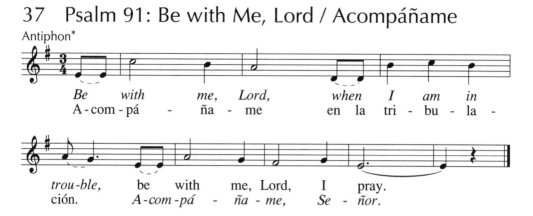

Be with me, Lord, when I am in
A-com-pá - ña-me en la tri-bu-la -

trou-ble, be with me, Lord, I pray.
ción. A-com-pá - ña-me, Se - ñor.

Verses

1. You who dwell in the shelter of the Lord, Most High,
   who abide in the shadow of our God,
   say to the Lord: "My refuge and fortress, the God in whom I trust."

2. No evil shall befall you, no pain come near,
   for the angels stand close by your side,
   guarding you always and bearing you gently, watching over your life.

3. Those who cling to the Lord live secure in God's love,
   lifted high, those who trust in God's name,
   call on the Lord who will never forsake you.
   God will bring you salvation and joy.

1. *Tú que vives al amparo del Altísimo, y descansas a la sombra de Dios,*
   dile_al Señor: "Mi refugio, mi_alcázar, Dios mío, confío en ti."

2. *Ni temor ni dolor a ti no te_alcanzará, pues sus ángeles a tu lado_están*
   siempre guardándote en tus caminos; te sostendrán en sus manos.

3. *El Señor guardará_a los que_en él confiarán,*
   porque ellos conocen su nombre;
   me_invocarán y les responderé; les hará ver su salvación.

*For a bilingual antiphon, sing the text in italics.

Text: Psalm 91:1–2, 10–11, 14–15, Marty Haugen; tr. by Ronald F. Krisman
Music: Marty Haugen
© 1980, tr. 2012, GIA Publications, Inc.

Antiphon*

The Lord is kind and mer-ci-ful, *the*
El Se - ñor es com - pa - si - vo y

Lord is kind and mer-ci-ful.
mi - se - ri - cor - dio - so.

Verses

1. Bless the Lord, O my soul, and all my being bless God's name;
   bless the Lord, and forget not God's benefits.

2. God pardons all your iniquities, and comforts your sorrows,
   redeems your life from destruction and crowns you with kindness.

3. Merciful, merciful, and gracious is our God;
   slow to anger, abounding in kindness.

1. *Bendice, alma mía, al santo nombre del Señor;*
   alábalo y no olvides sus favores.

2. *Perdona todas tus culpas y cura tus dolencias,*
   rescatándote de la tumba, y colmándote de gracia.

3. *Tierno, misericordioso es nuestro Dios;*
   lento a la ira, rico en clemencia.

For a bilingual antiphon, sing the text in italics.

Text: Psalm 103:1–2, 3–4, 8, Marty Haugen, © 1983, GIA Publications, Inc.; tr. by Ronald F. Krisman, © 2012, GIA Publications, Inc.;
English antiphon, *Lectionary for Mass*, © 1969, 1981, 1997, ICEL; Spanish antífona, *Leccionario, Edición Hispanoamérica*, © 1970, 1972,
Conferencia Episcopal Española
Music: Marty Haugen, © 1983, GIA Publications, Inc.

39 Psalm 103: The Lord Is Kind and Merciful

Antiphon

The Lord is kind and mer - ci - ful.

Text: *Lectionary for Mass,* © 1969, 1981, 1997, ICEL
Music: David Haas, © 1986, GIA Publications, Inc.

Verses

1. The LORD is compassionate and gracious,
   slow to anger and rich in mercy.
   He does not treat us according to our sins,
   nor repay us according to our faults.

2. As a father has compassion on his children,
   the LORD's compassion is on those who fear him.
   For he knows of what we are made;
   he remembers that we are dust.

3. Man, his days are like grass;
   he flowers like the flower of the field.
   The wind blows, and it is no more,
   and its place never sees it again.

4. But the mercy of the LORD is everlasting
   upon those who hold him in fear,
   upon children's children his justice,
   for those who keep his covenant.

Text: Psalm 103:8 and 10, 13–14, 15–16, 17–18a; *The Revised Grail Psalms,* © 2010, Conception Abbey and The Grail, admin. by GIA Publications, Inc.

40 Psalm 116: I Will Walk before the Lord

Antiphon

I will walk be-fore the Lord, in the land of the liv - ing.

Verses

1. How gracious is the LORD, and just;
   our God has compassion.
   The LORD protects the simple;
   I was brought low, and he saved me.

2. I trusted, even when I said,
   "I am sorely afflicted,"
   and when I said in my alarm,
   "These people are all liars."

3. How precious in the eyes of the LORD
   is the death of his faithful.
   Your servant, LORD, your servant am I,
   you have loosened my bonds.

Psalm 116: I Will Walk in the Presence   41

Antiphon

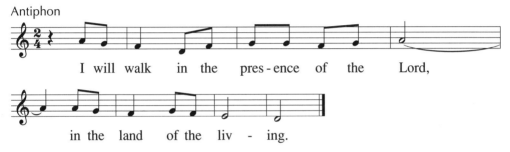

I will walk in the pres-ence of the Lord,

in the land of the liv - ing.

Verses

1. How gracious is the LORD, and just;
   our God has compassion.
   The LORD protects the simple;
   I was brought low, and he saved me.

2. I trusted, even when I said,
   "I am sorely afflicted,"
   and when I said in my alarm,
   "These people are all liars."

3. How precious in the eyes of the LORD
   is the death of his faithful.
   Your servant, LORD, your servant am I,
   you have loosened my bonds.

42 Psalm 122: Let Us Go Rejoicing

Antiphon

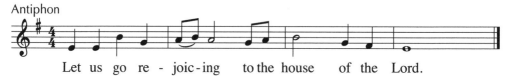

Let us go re - joic-ing to the house of the Lord.

Verses

1. I rejoiced when they said to me,
   "Let us go to the house of the LORD."
   And now our feet are standing
   within your gates, O Jerusalem.

2. Jerusalem is built as a city
   bonded as one together.
   It is there that the tribes go up,
   the tribes of the LORD.

3. For Israel's witness it is
   to praise the name of the LORD.
   There were set the thrones for judgment,
   the thrones of the house of David.

4. For the peace of Jerusalem pray,
   "May they prosper, those who love you."
   May peace abide in your walls,
   and security be in your towers.

5. For the sake of my family and friends,
   let me say, "Peace upon you."
   For the sake of the house of the LORD, our God,
   I will seek good things for you.

Text: Psalm 122; *The Revised Grail Psalms*, © 2010, Conception Abbey and The Grail, admin. by GIA Publications, Inc.;
antiphon, *Lectionary for Mass*, © 1969, 1981, 1997, ICEL
Music: Michel Guimont, © 1994, GIA Publications, Inc.

Psalm 122: I Rejoiced When I Heard Them Say   43

Antiphon

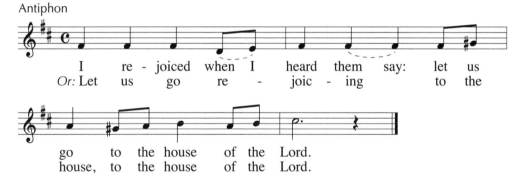

I re-joiced when I heard them say: let us
Or: Let us go re - joic - ing to the

go to the house of the Lord.
house, to the house of the Lord.

Text: *Lectionary for Mass,* © 1969, 1981, 1997, ICEL
Music: Robert J. Batastini, © 1975, GIA Publications, Inc.

Verses

1. I rejoiced when they said to me,
   "Let us go to the house of the LORD."
   And now our feet are standing
   within your gates, O Jerusalem.

2. Jerusalem is built as a city
   bonded as one together.
   It is there that the tribes go up,
   the tribes of the LORD.

3. For Israel's witness it is
   to praise the name of the LORD.
   There were set the thrones for judgment,
   the thrones of the house of David.

4. For the peace of Jerusalem pray,
   "May they prosper, those who love you."
   May peace abide in your walls,
   and security be in your towers.

5. For the sake of my family and friends,
   let me say, "Peace upon you."
   For the sake of the house of the LORD, our God,
   I will seek good things for you.

Text: Psalm 122; *The Revised Grail Psalms,* © 2010, Conception Abbey and The Grail, admin. by GIA Publications, Inc.

44　Psalm 130: Out of the Depths

Refrain

Out of the depths I cry to you, O Lord.

Verses

1. Out of the depths I cry to you;
   Lord, hear my voice!
   Let your ears be attentive
   to my prayer for help.

2. If you, O Lord,
   should mark our guilt,
   Lord, who could stand?
   But with you there is mercy,
   that you may be revered.

3. I put my trust in God, the Lord,
   trusting his word.
   My soul waits for the Lord
   more than sentinels wait for the dawn.

4. More than sentinels wait for the dawn,
   Israel waits for God.
   For with God there is kindness,
   and with God, plenteous redemption.

Text: Psalm 130:1–2, 3–4, 5–6, 7; Paul Melley
Music: Paul Melley
© 2008, GIA Publications, Inc.

45　Psalm 131: My Soul Is Still

Refrain

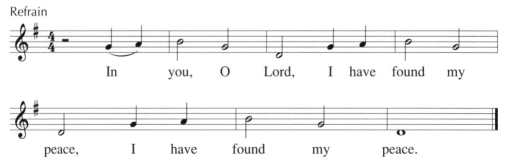

In you, O Lord, I have found my

peace, I have found my peace.

Verses

1. My heart is not proud, my eyes not above you;
   You fill my soul. I am not filled with great things,
   nor with thoughts beyond me.

2. My soul is still, my soul stays quiet,
   longing for you like a weaned child
   in its mother's arms; so is my soul a child with you.

Text: Psalm 131:1, 2; David Haas, © 1985, GIA Publications, Inc.; refrain, *Lectionary for Mass*, © 1969, 1981, 1997, ICEL
Music: David Haas, © 1985, GIA Publications, Inc.

Psalm 143: O Lord, Hear My Prayer   46

Antiphon

O Lord, hear my prayer, hear my prayer, O Lord.

Text: *Lectionary for Mass*, © 1969, 1981, 1997, ICEL
Music: Richard Proulx, © 1975, GIA Publications, Inc.

Verses

1. O LORD, listen to my prayer;
   turn your ear to my appeal.
   You are faithful, you are just; give answer.
   Do not call your servant to judgment,
   for in your sight no one living is justified.

2. I remember the days that are past;
   I ponder all your works.
   I muse on what your hand has wrought,
   and to you I stretch out my hands.
   Like a parched land my soul thirsts for you.

3. O LORD, make haste and answer me,
   for my spirit fails within me.
   In the morning, let me know your loving mercy,
   for in you I place my trust.

4. Teach me to do your will,
   for you are my God.
   Let your good spirit guide me
   upon ground that is level.

Text: Psalm 143:1–2, 5–6, 7ab and 8ab, 10; *The Revised Grail Psalms*, © 2010, Conception Abbey and The Grail, admin. by GIA Publications, Inc.
Music: Michel Guimont, © 1994, GIA Publications, Inc.

Service Music

47 GOSPEL ACCLAMATION

Al - le - lu - ia, al - le - lu - ia.

Al - le - lu - ia, al - le - lu - ia.

Music: Fintan O'Carroll, © 1985, GIA Publications, Inc.

48 GOSPEL ACCLAMATION

Al - le - lu - ia, al - le - lu - ia, al - le - lu - ia.

Al - le - lu - ia, al - le - lu - ia, al - le - lu - ia!

Music: Alleluia 7; Jacques Berthier, © 1984, Les Presses de Taizé, GIA Publications, Inc., agent

49 GOSPEL ACCLAMATION

Refrain

Al - le - lu - ia, al - le - lu - ia, al - le - lu - ia!
Lent: Glo-ry to you, O Word of God, Lord Je - sus Christ.

Text: ICEL, © 1969
Music: *Mass of Light,* David Haas, © 1988, GIA Publications, Inc.

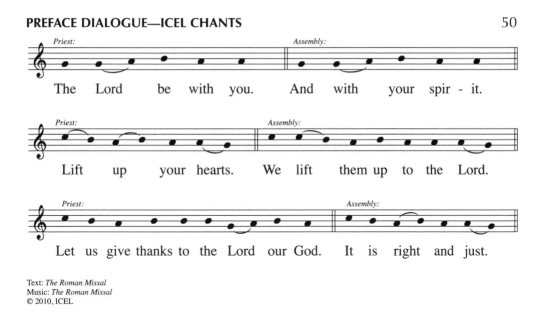

The Lord be with you. And with your spir - it.

Lift up your hearts. We lift them up to the Lord.

Let us give thanks to the Lord our God. It is right and just.

Text: *The Roman Missal*
Music: *The Roman Missal*
© 2010, ICEL

HOLY, HOLY, HOLY 51

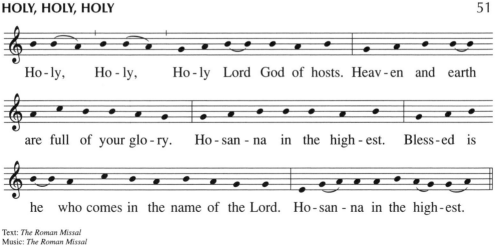

Ho - ly, Ho - ly, Ho - ly Lord God of hosts. Heav - en and earth

are full of your glo - ry. Ho - san - na in the high - est. Bless - ed is

he who comes in the name of the Lord. Ho - san - na in the high - est.

Text: *The Roman Missal*
Music: *The Roman Missal*
© 2010, ICEL

MEMORIAL ACCLAMATION A 52

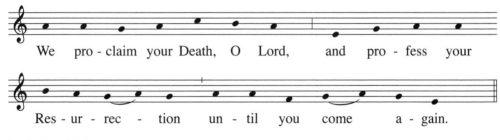

We pro - claim your Death, O Lord, and pro - fess your

Res - ur - rec - tion un - til you come a - gain.

Text: *The Roman Missal*
Music: *The Roman Missal*
© 2010, ICEL

53 MEMORIAL ACCLAMATION B

When we eat this Bread and drink this Cup, we pro-claim
your Death, O Lord, un-til you come a-gain.

Text: *The Roman Missal*
Music: *The Roman Missal*
© 2010, ICEL

54 MEMORIAL ACCLAMATION C

Save us, Sav-ior of the world, for by your Cross and
Res-ur-rec - tion you have set us free.

Text: *The Roman Missal*
Music: *The Roman Missal*
© 2010, ICEL

55 AMEN

A - men.   *Or:*   A - men, a - men, a - men.

56 THE LORD'S PRAYER

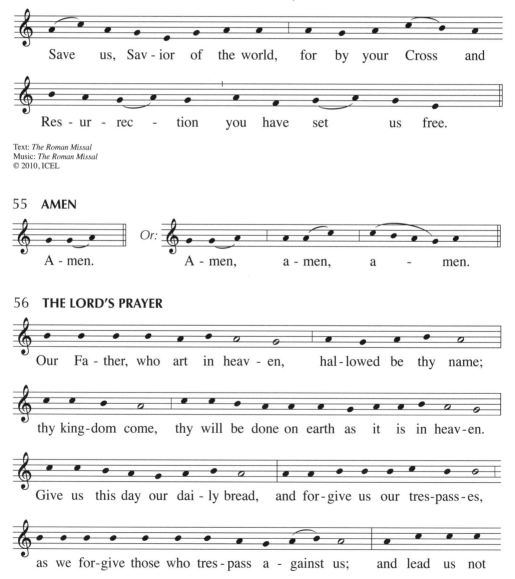

Our Fa - ther, who art in heav - en, hal-lowed be thy name;
thy king-dom come, thy will be done on earth as it is in heav-en.
Give us this day our dai - ly bread, and for-give us our tres-pass-es,
as we for-give those who tres-pass a - gainst us; and lead us not

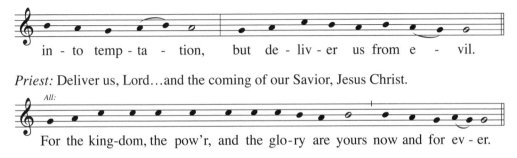

in - to temp - ta - tion, but de - liv - er us from e - vil.

Priest: Deliver us, Lord…and the coming of our Savior, Jesus Christ.

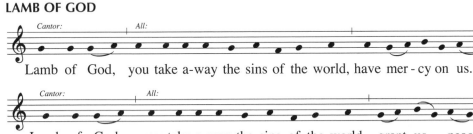

For the king-dom, the pow'r, and the glo-ry are yours now and for ev - er.

LAMB OF GOD 57

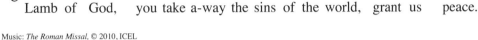

Lamb of God, you take a-way the sins of the world, have mer - cy on us.

Lamb of God, you take a-way the sins of the world, grant us peace.

HOLY, HOLY, HOLY—A COMMUNITY MASS 58

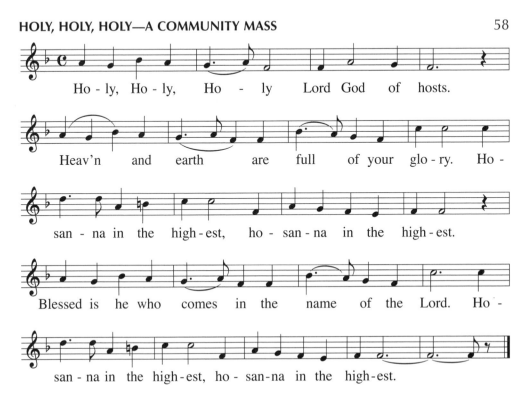

Ho - ly, Ho - ly, Ho - ly Lord God of hosts.

Heav'n and earth are full of your glo - ry. Ho -

san - na in the high-est, ho - san - na in the high - est.

Blessed is he who comes in the name of the Lord. Ho -

san - na in the high-est, ho - san-na in the high-est.

59 MEMORIAL ACCLAMATION A

We pro-claim your Death, O Lord, and pro-fess your Res-ur-rec-tion un-til you come a-gain.

Text: ICEL, © 2010
Music: *A Community Mass,* Richard Proulx, © 2010, GIA Publications, Inc.

60 AMEN

A-men, a-men, a-men.

Music: *A Community Mass,* Richard Proulx, © 1971, 1977, GIA Publications, Inc.

61 MEMORIAL ACCLAMATION B

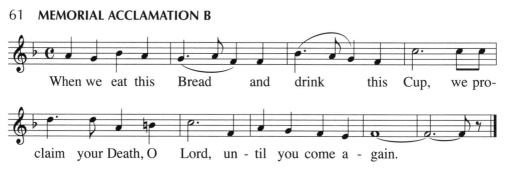

When we eat this Bread and drink this Cup, we pro-claim your Death, O Lord, un-til you come a-gain.

Text: ICEL, © 2010
Music: *A Community Mass,* Richard Proulx, © 1988, 2010, GIA Publications, Inc.

62 MEMORIAL ACCLAMATION C

Save us, Sav-ior of the world, for by your Cross and Res-ur-rec-tion you have set us free.

Text: ICEL, © 2010
Music: *A Community Mass,* Richard Proulx, © 1985, 2010, GIA Publications, Inc.

A - men, a - men, a - men.

Music: Danish Amen

LAMB OF GOD 64

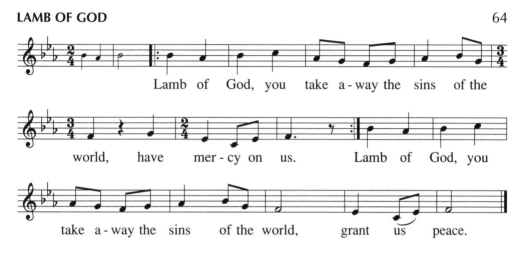

Lamb of God, you take a-way the sins of the

world, have mer-cy on us. Lamb of God, you

take a-way the sins of the world, grant us peace.

Music: *A Community Mass,* Richard Proulx, © 1971, 1977, GIA Publications, Inc.

HOLY, HOLY, HOLY—PEOPLE'S MASS 65

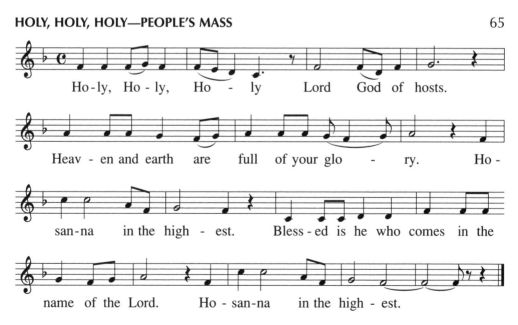

Ho-ly, Ho-ly, Ho - ly Lord God of hosts.

Heav - en and earth are full of your glo - ry. Ho -

san-na in the high - est. Bless-ed is he who comes in the

name of the Lord. Ho - san-na in the high - est.

Text: ICEL, © 2010
Music: *People's Mass,* Jan M. Vermulst; arr. and adapt. by Richard Proulx, © 1970, 1987, 2010, World Library Publications

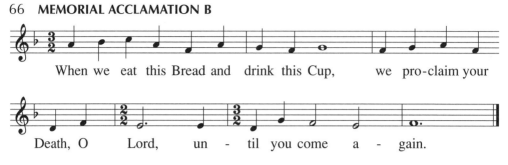

When we eat this Bread and drink this Cup, we pro-claim your
Death, O Lord, un - til you come a - gain.

Text: ICEL, © 2010
Music: *Danish Amen Mass*, David Kraehenbuehl; acc. by Charles G. Frischmann, © 1970, 1973, 2011, World Library Publications

67 **AMEN**

A - men, a - men, a - men.

Music: Danish Amen

68 **HOLY, HOLY, HOLY—MASS OF THE ANGELS AND SAINTS**

Ho - ly, Ho - ly, Ho - ly Lord God of hosts.

Heav'n and earth are full of your glo - ry. Ho -

san - na, ho - san - na, ho - san - na in the

high - est, ho - san - na, ho - san - na, ho -

san - na in the high - est. Bless - ed is he who comes in the

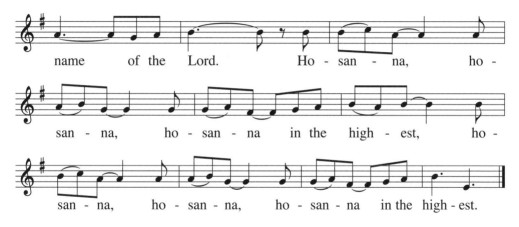

name of the Lord. Ho - san - na, ho -

san - na, ho - san - na in the high - est, ho -

san - na, ho - san - na, ho - san - na in the high - est.

Text: ICEL, © 2010
Music: *Mass of the Angels and Saints,* Steven R. Janco, © 1996, 2010, GIA Publications, Inc.

MEMORIAL ACCLAMATION A 69

We pro - claim your Death, O Lord, and pro -

fess your Res - ur - rec - tion un - til you come a - gain.

Text: ICEL, © 2010
Music: *Mass of the Angels and Saints,* Steven R. Janco, © 1996, 2010, GIA Publications, Inc.

MEMORIAL ACCLAMATION B 70

When we eat this Bread and drink this Cup,

we pro - claim your Death, O Lord, un - til you come a - gain.

Text: ICEL, © 2010
Music: *Mass of the Angels and Saints,* Steven R. Janco, © 1996, 2010, GIA Publications, Inc.

71 MEMORIAL ACCLAMATION C

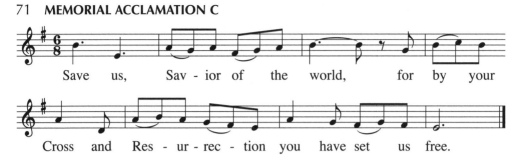

Save us, Sav - ior of the world, for by your
Cross and Res - ur - rec - tion you have set us free.

Text: ICEL, © 2010
Music: *Mass of the Angels and Saints*, Steven R. Janco, © 2010, GIA Publications, Inc.

72 AMEN

A - men, a - men, a - men.
A - men, a - men, a - men.

Music: *Mass of the Angels and Saints*, Steven R. Janco, © 1996, GIA Publications, Inc.

73 LAMB OF GOD

Cantor: Have mer - cy on us. *All:* Have mer - cy on us. *Repeat ad lib.*
Cantor: Grant us peace. *All:* Grant us peace.

Music: *Mass of the Angels and Saints*, Steven R. Janco, © 1996, GIA Publications, Inc.

Hymns and Songs

Amazing Grace! 74

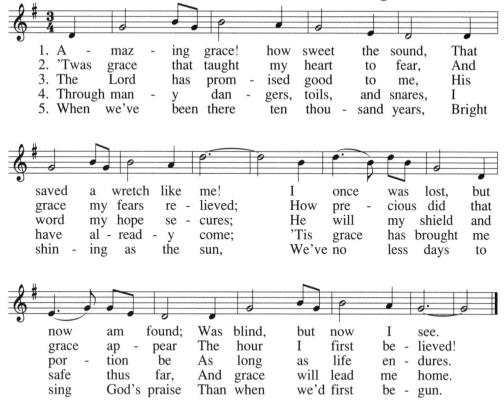

1. A - maz - ing grace! how sweet the sound, That
2. 'Twas grace that taught my heart to fear, And
3. The Lord has prom - ised good to me, His
4. Through man - y dan - gers, toils, and snares, I
5. When we've been there ten thou - sand years, Bright

saved a wretch like me! I once was lost, but
grace my fears re - lieved; How pre - cious did that
word my hope se - cures; He will my shield and
have al - read - y come; 'Tis grace has brought me
shin - ing as the sun, We've no less days to

now am found; Was blind, but now I see.
grace ap - pear The hour I first be - lieved!
por - tion be As long as life en - dures.
safe thus far, And grace will lead me home.
sing God's praise Than when we'd first be - gun.

Text: St. 1–4, John Newton, 1725–1807; st. 5, attr. to John Rees, fl.1859
Tune: NEW BRITAIN, CM; *Virginia Harmony,* 1831; arr. by Evelyn Simpson-Curenton, b.1953, © 2000, GIA Publications, Inc.

May Saints and Angels 75

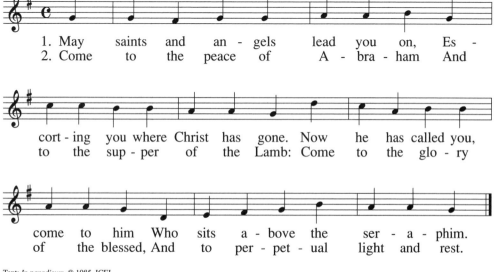

1. May saints and an - gels lead you on, Es -
2. Come to the peace of A - bra - ham And

cort - ing you where Christ has gone. Now he has called you,
to the sup - per of the Lamb: Come to the glo - ry

come to him Who sits a - bove the ser - a - phim.
of the blessed, And to per - pet - ual light and rest.

Text: *In paradisum,* © 1985, ICEL
Tune: TALLIS' CANON, LM; Thomas Tallis, c.1505-1585

76 Sing with All the Saints in Glory / Canten con Gloriosos Fieles

1. Sing with all the saints in glo - ry, Sing the res - ur -
2. O what glo - ry, far ex - ceed - ing All that eye has
3. Life e - ter - nal! heav'n re - joic - es: Je - sus lives who

1. Can - ten con glo - rio - sos fie - les Him - nos de re -
2. ¡Oh! qué glo - ria tan ex - cel - sa, Im - po - si - ble
3. Vi - da e - ter - na, ex - cla - ma el cie - lo; Vi - ve Cris - to

rec - tion song! Death and sor - row, earth's dark sto - ry,
yet per-ceived! Ho - liest hearts, for a - ges plead - ing,
once was dead. Shout with joy, O death - less voic - es!

su - rrec - ción. Muer - te y due - lo, tris - te his - to - ria,
con - ce - bir. Los más pu - ros co - ra - zo - nes
que mu - rió. ¡Gri - ten, vo - ces in - mor - ta - les!

To the for - mer days be - long. All a - round the
Nev - er that full joy con - ceived. God has prom - ised,
Child of God, lift up your head! Pa - tri - archs from

Pe - nas del pa - sa - do son. Nu - bes ne - gras
No es - pe - ra - ron re - ci - bir. Dios pro - me - te,
Al - cen ros - tros ha - cia Dios. Los pa - triar - cas

clouds are break - ing, Soon the storms of time shall cease; In God's
Christ pre - pares it, There on high our wel - come waits. Ev - 'ry
dis - tant a - ges, Saints all long - ing for their heav'n, Proph - ets,

se di - si - pan, La tor - men - ta ce - sa ya. Des - per -
Cris - to o - fre - ce El ban - que - te ce - les - tial. Pa - ra
del pa - sa - do, Los que es - pe - ran ce - le - brar, To - dos

like - ness we a - wak - en, Know - ing ev - er - last - ing peace.
hum - ble spir - it shares it; Christ has passed the e - ter - nal gates.
psalm - ists, seers, and sag - es, All a - wait the glo - ry giv'n.

tan - do en su i - ma - gen, Dios la e - ter - na paz nos da.
to - dos los hu - mil - des, Vi - da en Cris - to es e - ter - nal.
sa - bios y pro - fe - tas Glo - ria an - he - lan sin ce - sar.

4. Life eternal! O what wonders
   Crowd on faith; what joy unknown,
   When, amid earth's closing thunders,
   Saints shall stand before the throne!
   Oh, to enter that bright portal,
   See that glowing firmament,
   Know, with you, O God immortal,
   Jesus Christ whom you have sent!

4. ¡Vida eterna! ¡Gozo eterno!
   Fieles cantan a una voz.
   Cesan truenos y nos vemos
   Frente al trono tuyo, Dios.
   Y al pasar por tus portales,
   Brilla el cielo con fulgor.
   Celebramos tu venida
   En tu Hijo, el Salvador.

Text: 1 Corinthians 15:20; William J. Irons, 1812–1883, alt.; tr. by Alberto Merubia, b.1919, © 2010, GIA Publications, Inc.
Tune: HYMN TO JOY, 8 7 8 7 D; arr. from Ludwig van Beethoven, 1770–1827, by Edward Hodges, 1796–1867

The Strife Is O'er 77

Refrain

Al - le - lu - ia, al - le - lu - ia, al - le - lu - ia!

Verses

1. The strife is o'er, the bat - tle done;
2. The pow'rs of death have done their worst;
3. On the third day Christ rose a - gain,
4. He closed the yawn - ing gates of hell;
5. Lord, by the stripes which wound - ed you,

Now is the Vic - tor's tri - umph won! Songs of re -
But Christ their le - gions has dis - persed. Let shouts of
Glo - rious in maj - es - ty to reign. O let us
The bars from heav'n's high por - tals fell. Let hymns of
Free from death's sting your ser - vants too, That we may

D.C.

joic - ing have be - gun. Al - le - lu - ia!
ho - ly joy out - burst. Al - le - lu - ia!
swell the joy - ful strain. Al - le - lu - ia!
praise his tri - umph tell. Al - le - lu - ia!
live and sing to you. Al - le - lu - ia!

Text: Finita jam sunt praelia; Latin, 12th C.; tr. by Francis Pott, 1832–1909, alt.
Tune: VICTORY, 888 with alleluia and refrain; Giovanni da Palestrina, 1525–1594; adapt. by William H. Monk, 1823–1889

78 I Know That My Redeemer Lives! / Yo Sé Que Vive el Salvador

1. I know that my Re - deem - er lives!
2. He lives to bless me with his love;
3. He lives and grants me dai - ly breath;

1. Yo sé que vi - ve el Sal - va - dor:
2. Re - su - ci - tó con gran po - der;
3. Al vic - to - rio - so Re - den - tor,

What joy this blest as - sur - ance gives!
He lives to plead for me a - bove;
He lives, and I shall con - quer death;

Es de la muer - te_el Ven - ce - dor;
Glo - rio - so rei - na por do - quier;
Al gran - de_e - ter - no Ven - ce - dor,

He lives, he lives who once was dead;
He lives my hun - gry soul to feed;
He lives my man - sion to pre - pare;

Nin - gún te - mor ja - más ten - dré,
Con su fa - vor y ben - di - ción
Glo - ria_y lo - or le can - ta - ré

He lives, my ev - er - last - ing Head!
He lives to help in time of need.
He lives to bring me safe - ly there.

Pues a su la - do vi - vi - ré.
Sus - ten - ta - rá mi co - ra - zón.
Con gran a - mor y vi - va fe.

4. He lives, all glory to his name;
   He lives, my Savior, still the same;
   What joy this blest assurance gives:
   I know that my Redeemer lives!

4. Con mi Jesús seguro_estoy,
   Pues por su gracia salvo soy;
   ¡Mi vida_entrego con amor
   Al fiel servicio del Señor!

Text: Samuel Medley, 1738–1799; tr. by Leopoldo Gros, b.1925, © 1991, Concordia Publishing House, d/b/a Editorial Concordia
Tune: DUKE STREET, LM; John Hatton, c.1710–1793

1. I want to walk as a child of the light.
2. I want to see the bright-ness of God.
3. I'm look-ing for the com-ing of Christ.

I want to fol - low Je - sus.
I want to look at Je - sus.
I want to be with Je - sus.

God set the stars to give light to the world. The
Clear sun of right-eous-ness shine on my path And
When we have run with pa-tience the race, We

star of my life is Je - sus.
show me the way to the Fa - ther.
shall know the joy of Je - sus.

In him there is no dark - ness at all. The

night and the day are both a - like. The

Lamb is the light of the cit - y of God.

Shine in my heart, Lord Je - sus.

Text: Ephesians 5:8–10, Revelation 21:23, John 12:46, 1 John 1:5, Hebrews 12:1; Kathleen Thomerson, b.1934, © 1970, 1975, Celebration
Tune: HOUSTON, 10 7 10 8 9 9 10 7; Kathleen Thomerson, b.1934, © 1970, 1975, Celebration; acc. by Robert J. Batastini, b.1942, © 1987, GIA
  Publications, Inc.

80 Lord of All Hopefulness

1. Lord of all hope-ful-ness, Lord of all joy,
2. Lord of all ea-ger-ness, Lord of all faith,
3. Lord of all kind-li-ness, Lord of all grace,
4. Lord of all gen-tle-ness, Lord of all calm,

Whose trust, ev-er child-like, no cares could de-stroy,
Whose strong hands were skilled at the plane and the lathe,
Your hands swift to wel-come, your arms to em-brace,
Whose voice is con-tent-ment, whose pres-ence is balm,

Be there at our wak-ing, and give us, we pray,
Be there at our la-bors, and give us, we pray,
Be there at our hom-ing, and give us, we pray,
Be there at our sleep-ing, and give us, we pray,

Your bliss in our hearts, Lord, at the break of the day.
Your strength in our hearts, Lord, at the noon of the day.
Your love in our hearts, Lord, at the eve of the day.
Your peace in our hearts, Lord, at the end of the day.

Text: Jan Struther, 1901–1953, © 1931, Oxford University Press
Tune: SLANE, 10 11 11 12; Irish melody; harm. by Erik Routley, 1917–1982, © 1975, Hope Publishing Company

81 Requiem Aeternam

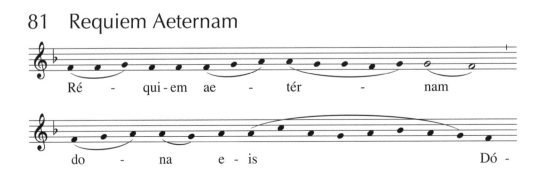

Ré - qui-em ae - tér - nam

do - na e - is Dó -

mi - ne; et lux per - pé - tu - a

lú - ce - at e - is.

Translation:
Eternal rest grant unto them, O Lord,
and may perpetual light shine upon them.

Text: *Requiem aeternam*
Music: Mode VI

O Lord, Hear My Prayer / Señor, Ten Piedad   82

Ostinato Refrain

O   Lord,   hear my prayer,   O Lord, hear my prayer:
Se - ñor,   ten pie - dad,   Se - ñor,   ten pie - dad:

when   I call   an - swer me.   O Lord, hear my prayer, O
si   te_in - vo - co,   ó - ye - me.   Se - ñor,   ten pie - dad, Se -

⌢ Last time

Lord, hear my prayer.   Come   and lis - ten   to me.   O
ñor,   ten pie - dad: Ven,   y_es - cu - cha   mi voz.   Se -

⌢ Last time

Text: Psalm 102; Taizé Community, 1982
Tune: Jacques Berthier, 1923–1994
© 1982, 2011, Les Presses de Taizé, GIA Publications, Inc., agent

83 We Remember

Refrain

We re-mem-ber how you loved us to your death,
and still we cel-e-brate, for you are with us here;
and we be-lieve that we will see you when you come
in your glo-ry, Lord. We re-mem-ber, we
cel-e-brate, we be-lieve.

Verses

1. Here, a mil-lion wound-ed souls Are
2. Now we re-cre-ate your love, We
3. Christ, the Fa-ther's great "A-men" To
4. See the face of Christ re-vealed In

yearn-ing just to touch you and be healed;
bring the bread and wine to share a meal:
all the hopes and dreams of ev-'ry heart,
ev-'ry per-son stand-ing by your side:

D.C.

Gath-er all your peo-ple, and hold them to your heart.
Sign of grace and mer-cy, the pres-ence of the Lord.
Peace be-yond all tell-ing, and free-dom from all fear.
Gifts to one an-oth-er, and tem-ples of your love.

Text: Marty Haugen, b.1950
Tune: WE REMEMBER, 7 10 12 with refrain; Marty Haugen, b.1950
© 1980, GIA Publications, Inc.

O God, Our Help in Ages Past / 84
Nuestra Esperanza y Protección

1. O God, our help in a - ges past, Our
2. Be - fore the hills in or - der stood, Or
3. A thou - sand a - ges in your sight Are
1. *Nues - tra_es - pe - ran - za_y pro - tec - ción Y*
2. *A - ún no_ha - bí - as la crea - ción For -*
3. *De - lan - te de tus o - jos son Mil*

hope for years to come, Our shel - ter from the
earth re - ceived its frame, From ev - er - last - ing
like an eve - ning gone, Short as the watch that
nues - tro_e - ter - no_ho - gar Has si - do, e - res
ma - do con bon - dad, Mas des - de la e -
a - ños, al pa - sar, Tan só - lo_un dí - a

storm - y blast, And our e - ter - nal home.
you are God, To end - less years the same.
ends the night Be - fore the ris - ing sun.
y se - rás Tan só - lo tú, Se - ñor.
ter - ni - dad Tú e - ras so - lo Dios.
que fu - gaz Fe - ne - ce con el sol.

4. Time, like an ever-rolling stream,
   Bears all our years away;
   They fly forgotten, as a dream
   Dies at the op'ning day.

4. *El tiempo corre_arrollador*
   Como_impetuoso mar;
   Y_así, cual sueño ves pasar
   Cada generación.

5. O God, our help in ages past,
   Our hope for years to come,
   Still be our guard while troubles last,
   And our eternal home.

5. *Nuestra_esperanza_y protección*
   Y nuestro_eterno_hogar,
   En la tormenta o_en la paz,
   Sé siempre tú, Señor.

Text: Psalm 90; Isaac Watts, 1674–1748, alt.; tr. by Federico J. Pagura, b.1923, © 1962
Tune: ST. ANNE, CM; attr. to William Croft, 1678–1727; harm. composite from 18th C. versions

85 On Eagle's Wings

Verse 3

3. You need not fear the ter-ror of the night, nor the ar-row that flies by day; though thou-sands fall a-bout you, near you it shall not come.

D.S.

Verse 4

4. For to his an-gels he's giv-en a com-mand to guard you in all of your ways; up-on their hands they will bear you up, lest you dash your foot a-gainst a stone.

D.S.

⊕ Coda

And hold you, hold you in the palm of his hand.

Text: Psalm 91; Michael Joncas, b.1951
Tune: Michael Joncas, b.1951
© 1979, OCP

1. I heard the voice of Je - sus say, "Come
2. I heard the voice of Je - sus say, "Be -
3. I heard the voice of Je - sus say, "I

un - to me and rest; Lay down, O wea - ry
hold, I free - ly give The liv - ing wa - ter;
am this dark world's light; Look un - to me, your

one, lay down Your head up - on my breast." I
thirst - y one, Stoop down and drink and live." I
morn shall rise, And all your day be bright." I

came to Je - sus as I was, So
came to Je - sus, and I drank Of
looked to Je - sus, and I found In

wea - ry, worn, and sad; I found in him a
that life - giv - ing stream; My thirst was quenched, my
him my star, my sun; And in that light of

rest - ing place, And he has made me glad.
soul re - vived, And now I live in him.
life I'll walk Till trav - 'ling days are done.

Text: Horatius Bonar, 1808–1889
Tune: KINGSFOLD, CMD; English melody; harm. by Ralph Vaughan Williams, 1872–1958

1. The King of love my shep - herd is, Whose good-ness
2. Where streams of liv - ing wa - ter flow, My ran-somed
3. Con - fused and fool - ish oft I strayed, But yet in
4. In death's dark vale I fear no ill With you, dear

1. *El Rey de a-mor es mi pas - tor, Su a - mor es*
2. *Me lle - va al fres - co ma - nan-tial, Ya bue - nos*
3. *Per - ver so y ne - cio* me a - par - té Por va - lles*
4. *En va - lle os - cu - ro no ten - dré Te - mor si*

fails me nev - er; I noth - ing lack if
soul he's lead - ing And, where the ver - dant
love he sought me, And on his shoul - der
Lord, be - side me, Your rod and staff my

ver - da - de - ro; Su am - pa - ro no me
pas - tos guí - a; No te - me - ré yo
pe - li - gro - sos; Me ha -lló, me tra - jo a
Dios me guí - a; Su va - ra y su ca -

I am his And he is mine for - ev - er.
pas - tures grow, With food ce - les - tial feed - ing.
gen - tly laid, And home, re - joic - ing, brought me.
com - fort still, Your cross be - fore to guide me.

fal - ta - rá, Pues yo soy su cor - de - ro.
nin - gún mal, Si mi pas - tor me cui - da.
su re - dil En hom - bros po - de - ro - sos.
ya - do son Cual luz al al - ma mí - a.

*Perversa y necia

5. You spread a table in my sight,
Your saving grace bestowing;
And, oh, what transport of delight
From your pure chalice flowing!

6. And so, through all the length of days
Your goodness fails me never;
Good Shepherd, may I sing your praise
Within your house forever.

5. *Ha puesto mesa para mí,*
Ungióme con aceite,
Mi copa rebosando está;
Su amor es mi deleite.

6. *Misericordia, gracia y paz*
Tú das al alma mía,
Y en tus mansiones moraré,
Señor, por largos días.

Text: Psalm 23; Henry W. Baker, 1821–1877, alt.; tr. by Frieda M. Hoh, 1896–1962
Tune: ST. COLUMBA, 8 7 8 7; Irish melody; harm. by A. Gregory Murray, OSB, 1905–1992, © Downside Abbey

88 Be Not Afraid

pow'r of hell and death is at your side,

D.S.

know that I am with you through it all.

Verse 3

3. Bless-ed are your poor, for the king-dom shall be

theirs. Blest are you that weep and mourn, for

one day you shall laugh. And if wick-ed tongues in-

sult and hate you all be-cause of me,

D.S.

bless-ed, bless-ed are you!

Text: Isaiah 43:2–3, Luke 6:20ff; Bob Dufford, SJ, b.1943
Tune: Bob Dufford, SJ, b.1943; acc. by Theophane Hytrek, OSF, 1915–1992

89 Eye Has Not Seen

Refrain

Eye has not seen, ear has not heard what God has read-y for those who love him; Spir-it of love, come, give us the mind of Je - sus, teach us the wis-dom of God.

Verses 1-3

1. When pain and sor - row weigh us down, be near to us, O
2. Our lives are but a sin - gle breath, we flow-er and we
3. To those who see with eyes of faith, the Lord is ev - er

Lord; for - give the weak - ness of our faith, and
fade, yet all our days are in your hands, so
near, re - flect - ed in the fac - es of

D.C.

bear us up with - in your peace-ful word.
we re - turn in love what love has made.
all the poor and low - ly of the world.

Verse 4

4. We sing a mys-t'ry from the past in halls where saints have

trod,   yet   ev - er new   the   mu - sic rings to

D.C.

Je - sus, Liv - ing   Song   of   God.

Text: 1 Corinthians 2:9–10; Marty Haugen, b.1950
Tune: Marty Haugen, b.1950
© 1982, GIA Publications, Inc.

What Wondrous Love Is This   90

1. What   won - drous love   is   this,   O my   soul,   O   my   soul!
2. To   God   and   to   the Lamb   I   will   sing,   I   will   sing;
3. And   when from death I'm   free,   I'll sing   on,   I'll sing   on;

What   won - drous love   is   this,   O   my   soul!
To   God   and   to   the   Lamb   I   will   sing.
And   when from death I'm   free,   I'll   sing   on.

What   won - drous love   is   this   that   caused the   Lord of   bliss
To   God   and   to   the   Lamb, who   is   the   great I   AM,
And   when from death I'm   free,   I'll   sing and   joy - ful   be,

To   bear   the dread - ful   curse   for   my   soul,   for   my   soul;
While   mil - lions join the   theme,   I   will   sing,   I   will   sing;
And   through e - ter - ni - ty   I'll sing   on,   I'll sing   on;

To   bear   the dread - ful   curse   for   my   soul!
While   mil - lions join the   theme,   I   will   sing.
And   through e - ter - ni - ty   I'll sing   on.

Text: Alexander Means, 1801–1883
Tune: WONDROUS LOVE, 12 9 12 12 9; *Southern Harmony*, 1835; harm. by Richard Proulx, 1937–2010, © 1975, GIA Publications, Inc.

91 You Are Mine / Contigo Estoy

Verses

1. I will come to you in the si - lence,
2. I am hope for all who are hope - less,
3. I am strength for all the de - spair - ing,
4. am the Word that leads all to free - dom, I

1. Te ha - bla - ré en la paz del si - len - cio,
2. es - pe - ran - za de quien an - he - la, la
3. Soy la for - ta - le - za del dé - bil;
4. Soy pa - la - bra li - be - ra - do - ra, la

I will lift you from all your fear.
I am eyes for all who long to see. In the
heal - ing for the ones who dwell in shame.
am the peace the world can - not give.

y del mie - do te li - bra - ré. Mi
vis - ta de los que no pue - den ver.
al a - ver - gon - za - do e - xal - ta - ré. Los
paz que el mun - do no pue - de dar. Tu

You will hear my voice, I claim you as my choice, be
shad - ows of the night, I will be your light,
All the blind will see, the lame will all run free, and
I will call your name, em - brac - ing all your pain. Stand

voz es - cu - cha - rás, y mí - o tú se - rás.
Con in - ten - si - dad bri - lla - ré en la os-cu - ri - dad.
cie - gos ve - rán, los li - sia - dos co - rre - rán. Mi
nom - bre lla - ma - ré; tu llan - to to - ma - ré. Le -

still and know I am here. *(To verse 2)*
come and rest in me. *(To refrain)*
all will know my name. *(To refrain)*
up, now walk, and live! *(To refrain)*

Jun - to a ti es - ta - ré. (A la estrofa 2) 2. Soy
Tu des-can - so quie - ro ser. (Al estribillo)
nom - bre re - ve - la - ré. (Al estribillo)
ván - ta - te a ca - mi - nar. (Al estribillo)

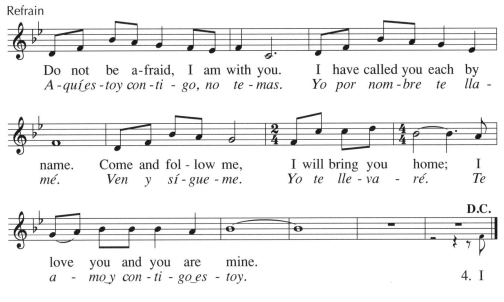

Do not be a-fraid, I am with you. I have called you each by
A-quíes-toy con-ti-go, no te-mas. Yo por nom-bre te lla-

name. Come and fol-low me, I will bring you home; I
mé. Ven y sí-gue-me. Yo te lle-va-ré. Te

love you and you are mine.
a - mo_y con-ti-go_es-toy.

D.C.

4. I

Text: David Haas, b.1957; tr. by Santiago Fernández, b.1971
Tune: David Haas, b.1957
© 1991, tr. 2005, GIA Publications, Inc.

Lord Our God, Receive Your Servant 92

Refrain

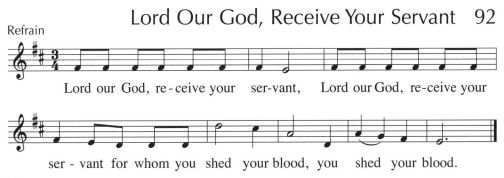

Lord our God, re-ceive your ser-vant, Lord our God, re-ceive your

ser-vant for whom you shed your blood, you shed your blood.

Verses

1. Remember, Lord, that we are dust,
   like grass, like a flow'r of the field.
   One moment we burst into bloom,
   then vanish, vanish for ever.

2. Saints of God, come to his/her aid,
   bid him/her welcome, you angels of the Lord.
   Receive, receive his/her soul
   and present him/her to God the Most High.

3. Now let eternal rest be granted to him/her, O Lord;
   and let perpetual light shine, shine upon him/her.

Text: Adapted from *Order of Christian Funerals*; John L. Bell
Music: John L. Bell
© 1996, Iona Community, GIA Publications, Inc., agent

93 Jesus, Lead the Way

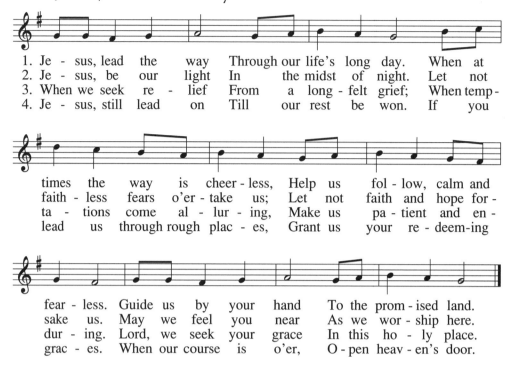

1. Je - sus, lead the way Through our life's long day. When at
2. Je - sus, be our light In the midst of night. Let not
3. When we seek re - lief From a long - felt grief; When temp -
4. Je - sus, still lead on Till our rest be won. If you

times the way is cheer - less, Help us fol - low, calm and
faith - less fears o'er - take us; Let not faith and hope for -
ta - tions come al - lur - ing, Make us pa - tient and en -
lead us through rough plac - es, Grant us your re - deem - ing

fear - less. Guide us by your hand To the prom - ised land.
sake us. May we feel you near As we wor - ship here.
dur - ing. Lord, we seek your grace In this ho - ly place.
grac - es. When our course is o'er, O - pen heav - en's door.

Text: *Jesu, geh voran;* Nicholas L. von Zinzendorf, 1700–1760; tr. by Jane Borthwick, 1813–1897, alt.
Tune: ROCHELLE, 55 88 55; Adam Drese, 1620–1701; harm. alt.

94 Jesus, Remember Me

Ostinato Refrain

Je - sus, re - mem - ber me when you come in - to your King - dom.
Spanish: Je - sús, re - cuér - da - me cuan - do en - tres en tu Rei - no.
Polish: Je - zu, w kró - les - twie Twym wspom - nij na swo - je - go słu - gę.

Je - sus, re - mem - ber me when you come in - to your King - dom.
Je - sús, re - cuér - da - me, cuan - do en - tres en tu Rei - no.
Je - zu, w kró - les - twie Twym wspom - nij na swo - je - go słu - gę.

Text: Luke 23:42; Taizé Community, 1981
Tune: Jacques Berthier, 1923–1994
© 1981, 2005, Les Presses de Taizé, GIA Publications, Inc., agent

1. Soon and ver-y soon we are goin' to see the King,
2. No more cry-in' there, we are goin' to see the King,
3. No more dy-in' there, we are goin' to see the King,
4. Soon and ver-y soon we are goin' to see the King,

Soon and ver-y soon we are goin' to see the King,
No more cry-in' there, we are goin' to see the King,
No more dy-in' there, we are goin' to see the King,
Soon and ver-y soon we are goin' to see the King,

Soon and ver-y soon we are goin' to see the King.
No more cry-in' there, we are goin' to see the King.
No more dy-in' there, we are goin' to see the King. Hal-le-
Soon and ver-y soon we are goin' to see the King.

1., 2.
lu - jah, hal-le-lu - jah, we're goin' to see the King!

3., 4.
Hal - le - lu - jah, hal - le - lu -

jah, hal - le - lu - jah, hal - le - lu - jah.

Text: Andraé Crouch, b.1942
Tune: SOON AND VERY SOON, 12 12 12 14; Andraé Crouch, b.1942
© 1976, Crouch Music/Bud John Songs, admin. at EMICMGPublishing.com

96 Blest Are They / Benditos los Pobres

Verses 1–3

1. Blest are they, the poor in spir - it;
2. Blest are they, the low - ly ones;
3. Blest are they who show mer - cy;

1. Ben - di - tos los po - bres en el es - pí - ri - tu,
2. Ben - di - tos son los pa - cien - tes,
3. Ben - di - tos son los com - pa - si - vos,

theirs is the king - dom of God.
they shall in - her - it the earth.
mer - cy shall be theirs.

su - yo_es el rei - no de Dios. Di -
he - re - da - rán la tie - rra. Di -
ob - ten - drán pie - dad. Di -

Blest are they, full of sor - row;
Blest are they who hun - ger and thirst;
Blest are they, the pure of heart;

cho - sos son los que llo - ran,
cho - sos los que tie - nen sed y ham - bre,
cho - sos los lim - pios de co - ra - zón,

they shall be con - soled.
they shall have their fill.
they shall see God.

re - ci - bi - rán con - sue - lo.
por - que se - rán sa - cia - dos.
e - llos ve - rán a Dios.

Refrain

Re - joice and be glad! Bless - ed are
¡A - lé - gren - se y con - tén - ten - se! ¡Son los ben -

you, ho-ly are you! Re-joice and be glad!
di - tos de nues-tro Dios! ¡A - lé-gren-se y con-tén-ten-se!

Yours is the king-dom of God!
¡Su - yo_es el rei - no de Dios!

Verses 4, 5

4. ⸘ Blest are they who seek peace;
5. ⸘ Blest are you who suf - fer hate,
4. Ben - di - tos los que por la paz tra - ba-jan,
5. Ben - di - tos son los per - se - gui-dos,

they are the chil - dren of God.
all be - cause of me. Re -
e - llos son hi - jos de Dios. Di -
to - do por cau - sa mí - a. ¡A -

Blest are they who suf - fer in faith; the
joice and be glad, yours is the king - dom;
cho - sos los que por la fe su - fren,
lé - gren - se! Su re - com - pen - sa

To refrain

glo - ry of God is theirs.
shine for all to see.
su - ya_es la glo - ria de Dios.
gran-de_en el cie - lo se - rá.

Text: Matthew 5:3–12; David Haas, b.1957, tr. by Ronald F. Krisman, b.1946
Tune: David Haas, b.1957; vocal arr. by David Haas and Michael Joncas, b.1951
© 1985, tr. 2005, GIA Publications, Inc.

97 Keep in Mind

Refrain

Keep in mind that Je-sus Christ has died for us and is ris-en from the dead. He is our sav-ing Lord, he is joy for all a - ges.

Verse 1 *D.C.*

1. If we die with the Lord, we shall live with the Lord.
   If we en-dure with the Lord, we shall reign with the Lord.

Verses 2, 3 *D.C.*

2. In Christ all our sor - row, in Christ all our joy.
   In him hope of glo - ry, in him all our love.
3. In Christ our re - demp - tion, in Christ all our grace.
   In him our sal - va - tion, in him all our peace.

Text: 2 Timothy 2:8–12, Lucien Deiss, CSSp, 1921–2007
Tune: Lucien Deiss, CSSp, 1921–2007
© 1965, World Library Publications

98 Be Still and Know

Canon

1. 2. 3. 4.
Be still and know that I am God.

Be still and know that I am God.

Text: Psalm 46:10; John L. Bell, b.1949
Tune: John L. Bell, b.1949
© 1989, Iona Community, GIA Publications, Inc., agent

1. Shall we gath-er at the riv - er, Where bright
2. On the mar-gin of the riv - er, Wash - ing
3. Ere we reach the shin-ing riv - er, Lay we
4. Soon we'll reach the shin-ing riv - er, Soon our

an - gel feet have trod, With its crys - tal tide for
up its sil - ver spray, We will walk and wor - ship
ev - 'ry bur - den down; Grace our spir - its will de -
pil - grim-age will cease; Soon our hap - py hearts will

ev - er Flow-ing by the throne of God?
ev - er, All the hap - py gold - en day.
liv - er, And pro - vide a robe and crown.
quiv - er With the mel - o - dy of peace.

Yes, we'll gath - er at the riv - er, The beau - ti - ful, the

beau - ti - ful riv - er, Gath - er with the saints at the

riv - er That flows by the throne of God.

Text: Robert Lowry, 1826–1899
Tune: HANSON PLACE, 8 7 8 7 with refrain; Robert Lowry, 1826–1899

Sal - ve Re - gí - na,   ma - ter mi - se - ri - cór - di - ae:
Hail, Queen of Heav - en,   hail, our Moth - er com - pas - sion - ate,

Vi - ta, dul - cé - do   et spes no - stra sal - ve.
True life and com - fort   and our hope, we greet you!

Ad te cla - má - mus,   éx - su - les fí - li - i He - vae.
To you we ex - iles,   chil - dren of Eve, raise our voic - es.

Ad te sus - pi - rá - mus,   ge - mén - tes et flen - tes
We send up sighs to you,   as mourn - ing and weep - ing,

in hac la - cri - má - rum val - le.   E - ia er - go,
we pass through this vale of sor - row.   Then turn to us,

ad - vo - cá - ta no - stra,   il - los tu - os
O most gra - cious Wom - an,   those eyes of yours,

mi - se - ri - cór - des ó - cu - los   ad nos con - vér - te.
so full of love and ten - der - ness,   so full of pit - y.

Et Je - sum, be - ne - dí - ctum fru - ctum ven - tris tu - i,
And grant us af - ter these, our days of lone - ly ex - ile,

no - bis post hoc ex - sí - li - um o - stén - de.
the sight of your blest Son and Lord, Christ Je - sus.

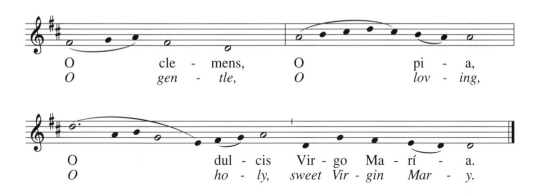

O cle - mens, O pi - a,
O gen - tle, O lov - ing,

O dul - cis Vir - go Ma - rí - a.
O ho - ly, sweet Vir - gin Mar - y.

Baptized in Water 101

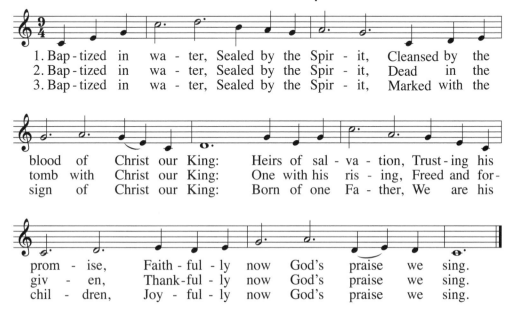

1. Bap - tized in wa - ter, Sealed by the Spir - it, Cleansed by the
2. Bap - tized in wa - ter, Sealed by the Spir - it, Dead in the
3. Bap - tized in wa - ter, Sealed by the Spir - it, Marked with the

blood of Christ our King: Heirs of sal - va - tion, Trust - ing his
tomb with Christ our King: One with his ris - ing, Freed and for -
sign of Christ our King: Born of one Fa - ther, We are his

prom - ise, Faith - ful - ly now God's praise we sing.
giv - en, Thank - ful - ly now God's praise we sing.
chil - dren, Joy - ful - ly now God's praise we sing.

102   Litany of the Saints

Cantor: *Assembly:*

Lord, have mer - cy.   Lord, have mer - cy.
Christ, have mer - cy.   Christ, have mer - cy.
Lord, have mer - cy.   Lord, have mer - cy.

Cantor: *Assembly:*

		pray	for	us.
Holy Mary, Mother of	God,	pray	for	us.
Saint	Mich - ael,	pray	for	us.
Holy Angels of	God,	pray	for	us.
Saint John the	Bap - tist,	pray	for	us.
Saint	Jo - seph,	pray	for	us.
Saint Peter and Saint	Paul,	pray	for	us.
Saint	An - drew,	pray	for	us.
Saint	John,	pray	for	us.
Saint Mary	Mag - dalene,	pray	for	us.
Saint	Ste - phen,	pray	for	us.
Saint Ignatius of	An - tioch,	pray	for	us.
Saint	Law - rence,	pray	for	us.
Saint Perpetua and Saint Fe -	lic - ity,	pray	for	us.
Saint	Ag - nes,	pray	for	us.
Saint	Gre - gory,	pray	for	us.
Saint Au -	gus - tine,	pray	for	us.
Saint Atha -	na - sius,	pray	for	us.
Saint	Ba - sil,	pray	for	us.
Saint	Mar - tin,	pray	for	us.
Saint	Ben - edict,	pray	for	us.
Saint Francis and Saint	Dom - inic,	pray	for	us.
Saint Francis	Xa - vier,	pray	for	us.
Saint John Vi -	an - ney,	pray	for	us.
Saint Catherine of Si -	e - na,	pray	for	us.
Saint Teresa of	Je - sus,	pray	for	us.
All holy men and women, Saints of God,		pray	for	us.

Cantor: *Assembly:*

Christ, hear us.   Christ, hear us.

Cantor: *Assembly:*

Christ, gra - cious - ly hear us.   Christ, gra - cious - ly hear us.

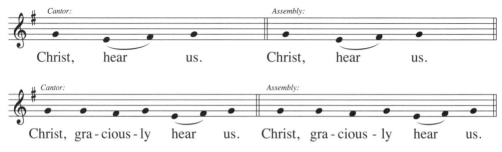

Text: *Litany of the Saints, Roman Missal*
Music: *Litany of the Saints, Roman Missal*
© 2010, ICEL

1. Ye watch-ers and ye ho-ly ones, Bright
2. O high-er than the cher-u-bim, More
3. Re-spond, ye souls in end-less rest, Ye
4. O friends, in glad-ness let us sing, Su-

ser-aphs, cher-u-bim, and thrones, Raise the
glo-rious than the ser-a-phim, Lead their
pa-tri-archs and proph-ets blest: "Al-le-
per-nal an-thems ech-o-ing: "Al-le-

glad strain: "Al-le-lu-ia!" Cry out, do-min-ions, prince-doms,
prais-es: "Al-le-lu-ia!" O bear-er of the e-ter-nal
lu-ia, Al-le-lu-ia!" Ye ho-ly twelve, ye mar-tyrs
lu-ia, Al-le-lu-ia!" To God the Fa-ther, God the

pow'rs, Vir-tues, arch-an-gels, an-gels' choirs:
Word, Most gra-cious, mag-ni-fy the Lord:
strong, All saints tri-um-phant, raise the song:
Son, And God the Spir-it, Three in One:

"Al-le-lu-ia! Al-le-lu-ia!" Al-le-lu-ia,

al-le-lu-ia, al-le-lu-ia!

Text: John A. Riley, 1858–1945
Tune: LASST UNS ERFREUEN, LM with alleluias; *Geistliche Kirchengesänge*, Cologne, 1623; harm. by Ralph Vaughan Williams, 1872–1958

104 Jerusalem, My Happy Home

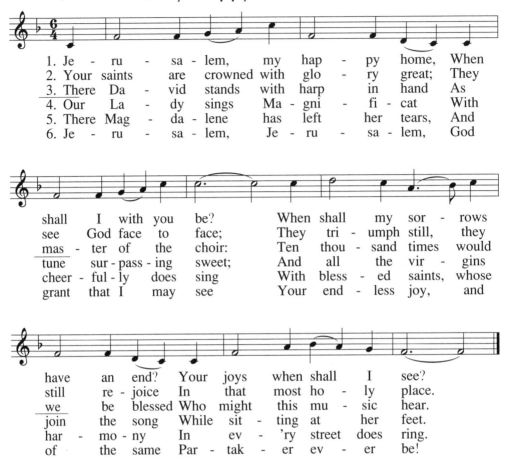

1. Je - ru - sa - lem, my hap - py home, When
2. Your saints are crowned with glo - ry great; They
3. There Da - vid stands with harp in hand As
4. Our La - dy sings Ma - gni - fi - cat With
5. There Mag - da - lene has left her tears, And
6. Je - ru - sa - lem, Je - ru - sa - lem, God

shall I with you be? When shall my sor - rows
see God face to face; They tri - umph still, they
mas - ter of the choir: Ten thou - sand times would
tune sur - pass - ing sweet; And all the vir - gins
cheer - ful - ly does sing With bless - ed saints, whose
grant that I may see Your end - less joy, and

have an end? Your joys when shall I see?
still re - joice In that most ho - ly place.
we be blessed Who might this mu - sic hear.
join the song While sit - ting at her feet.
har - mo - ny In ev - 'ry street does ring.
of the same Par - tak - er ev - er be!

Text: F.B.P., 16th C., alt.
Tune: LAND OF REST, CM; American melody; harm. by Richard Proulx, 1937–2010, © 1975, GIA Publications, Inc.

105 Lux Aeternam

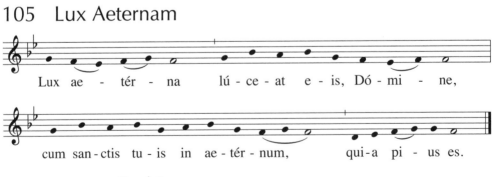

Lux ae - tér - na lú - ce - at e - is, Dó - mi - ne,

cum san - ctis tu - is in ae - tér - num, qui - a pi - us es.

Translation:
May eternal light shine upon them, O Lord,
in the company of your saints for eternity,
for you are full of goodness.

Text: *Lux aeterna*
Music: Mode VIII

1. For all the saints, who from their la - bors rest,
2. You were their rock, their for - tress and their might;
3. O may your sol - diers, faith - ful, true, and bold,
4. O blest com - mun - ion, fel - low - ship di - vine!
5. And when the strife is fierce, the war - fare long,
6. The gold - en eve - ning bright - ens in the west;

Who to the world their faith in you con - fessed; Your
You, Lord, their Cap - tain in the well - fought fight;
Fight as the saints who no - bly fought of old, And
We fee - bly strug - gle, they in glo - ry shine; Yet
Steals on the ear the dis - tant tri - umph song, And
Soon, soon to faith - ful war - riors comes their rest;

name, O Je - sus, be for - ev - er blest.
You, in the dark - ness drear, their one true light.
win with them the vic - tor's crown of gold.
all are one with - in your great de - sign.
hearts are brave a - gain, and arms are strong.
Sweet is the calm of par - a - dise the blest.

Al - le - lu - ia! Al - le - lu - ia!

7. But then there breaks a yet more glorious day;
   The saints triumphant rise in bright array;
   The King of glory passes on his way.
   Alleluia! Alleluia!

8. From earth's wide bounds, from ocean's farthest coast,
   Through gates of pearl streams in the countless host,
   Singing to Father, Son, and Holy Ghost:
   Alleluia! Alleluia!

Text: William W. How, 1823–1897, alt.
Tune: SINE NOMINE, 10 10 10 with alleluias; Ralph Vaughan Williams, 1872–1958

107 Alleluia! Sing to Jesus!

1. Alleluia! Sing to Jesus! His the scepter, his the throne. Alleluia! His the triumph, His the victory alone. Hark! The songs of peaceful Zion Thunder like a mighty flood: "Jesus out of ev'ry nation Has redeemed us by his blood."

2. Alleluia! Not as orphans Are we left in sorrow now; Alleluia! He is near us; Faith believes, nor questions how. Though the cloud from sight received him When the forty days were o'er, Shall our hearts forget his promise: "I am with you evermore"?

3. Alleluia! Bread of angels, Here on earth our food, our stay! Alleluia! Here the sinful Flee to you from day to day. Intercessor, friend of sinners, Earth's redeemer, plead for me, Where the songs of all the sinless Sweep across the crystal sea.

4. Alleluia! King eternal, You the Lord of lords we own; Alleluia! Born of Mary, Earth your footstool, heav'n your throne. You within the veil have entered, Robed in flesh, our great high priest; You on earth both priest and victim In the eucharistic feast.

Text: Revelation 5:9; William C. Dix, 1837–1898
Tune: HYFRYDOL, 8 7 8 7 D; Rowland H. Prichard, 1811–1887

Refrain

I re - ceive the liv - ing God, and my
Yo re - ci - bo al vi - vo Dios, y mi es -

heart is full of joy. I re - ceive the liv - ing
pí - ri - tu se a - le - gra. Yo re - ci - bo al vi - vo

God, and my heart is full of joy.
Dios, y mi es - pí - ri - tu se a - le - gra.

Verses

1. Je - sus says: I am the Bread Sent to
2. Je - sus says: I am the Vine, Far from
3. Je - sus says: I am the Way, And my
1. Di - ce Je - sús: Yo soy el Pan Que les
2. Di - ce Je - sús: Yo soy la Vid; Mi sar -
3. Di - ce Je - sús: Soy el Ca - mi - no, Y te an -

you from God Most High. Take and eat, and you will
whom no life can grow. If you join your - self to
path is straight and true. Fol - low me to where I
doy pa - ra nu - trir. Cuan - do co - mes de es - te
mien - to tú se - rás. Per - ma - ne - ce tú en
he - la mi buen Pa - dre. Si me si - gues, te guia -

D.C.

live; You need nev - er fear to die.
me, A rich har - vest you will know.
lead; There my Fa - ther waits for you.
pan, No hay ya mie - do de mo - rir.
mí: Mu - cho fru - to a - sí da - rás.
ré A tu ga - lar - dón ce - les - te.

*Cue notes are for Spanish verses 3, 5, 6, 8 and 9.

4. Jesus says: I am the Truth.
   If you follow close to me,
   You will know me in your heart,
   And my word will make you free.

4. *Dice Jesús: Soy la Verdad.*
   Sígueme con lealtad.
   Mi palabra guarda en ti:
   Ella es tu libertad.

5. Jesus says: I am the Life,
   Raised in triumph from the dead.
   As one Body now remain,
   Members joined to me, the Head.

5. *Dice Jesús: La Vida soy.*
   Por mi cruz no morirás.
   Como miembro de mi Cuerpo
   Vida nueva tú tendrás.

6. Jesus says: I am the Day,
   Shining brightly through your night.
   Welcome me, and you will walk
   By the Spirit's guiding light.

6. *Dice Jesús: Yo soy la Luz,*
   Que en la noche se aparece.
   Si me aceptas, cambiarás
   Por mi Espíritu celeste.

7. Jesus says: I am the Love
   Which can bind you close to me.
   Those who know this gift I bring
   Will find true community.

7. *Dice Jesús: Soy el Amor,*
   Sola fuente de unidad.
   Los que me recibirán
   Hallarán comunidad.

8. Jesus says: I am the Peace
   Which the world cannot bestow.
   Learn to love and live in me,
   And in you my Reign will grow.

8. *Dice Jesús: Yo soy la Paz*
   Que no puede dar el mundo.
   El que me ama vive en paz
   Y es testigo de mi reino.

9. Jesus says: I am the Lamb,
   And my death set sinners free.
   Those who drink the cup I drink
   Must take up this work with me.

9. *Dice Jesús: Soy el Cordero*
   Que murió por el pecado.
   El que bebe de mi Sangre
   Sigue haciendo mi trabajo.

Text: Vss. 1–3, 5–9, Bernard Geoffroy, b.1946; vss. 1–3, 5–9 English and all Spanish tr. by Ronald F. Krisman, b.1946, © 2011, 2012, GIA Publications, Inc.; vs. 4 English, anonymous
Tune: LIVING GOD, 7 7 7 7 with refrain; Dom Clément Jacob, OSB, 1906–1977, adapt.; harm. by Richard Proulx, 1937–2010, © 1986, GIA Publications, Inc.

Resurrection Song 110

Verse 1

1. Just as in Adam all die, so in Christ all will come to life again.

Response

A - men, a - men, a - men.

Verses 2, 3

2. God so loved the world that he gave his only Son,
   that whoever believes in him may not die, but have eternal life.

3. Grant them eternal rest, Lord,
   and fill their souls with resplendent light. Alleluia, alleluia.

Text: Based on 1 Corinthians 15:22; John 3:16
Tune: C. Alexander Peloquin, 1918–1997
© 1972, GIA Publications, Inc.

111 You Satisfy the Hungry Heart

Refrain

You sat-is-fy the hun-gry heart With gift of fin-est wheat; Come give to us, O sav-ing Lord, The bread of life to eat.

Verses

1. As when the shep - herd calls his sheep, They
2. With joy - ful lips we sing to you Our
3. Is not the cup we bless and share The
4. The mys - t'ry of your pres - ence, Lord, No
5. You give your - self to us, O Lord; Then

know and heed his voice; So when you call your
praise and grat - i - tude, That you should count us
blood of Christ out - poured? Do not one cup, one
mor - tal tongue can tell: Whom all the world can -
self - less let us be, To serve each oth - er

D.C.

fam - 'ly, Lord, We fol - low and re - joice.
wor - thy, Lord, To share this heav'n - ly food.
loaf, de - clare Our one - ness in the Lord?
not con - tain Comes in our hearts to dwell.
in your name In truth and char - i - ty.

Text: Omer Westendorf, 1916–1997
Tune: BICENTENNIAL, CM with refrain; Robert E. Kreutz, 1922–1996
© 1977, Archdiocese of Philadelphia. Published by International Liturgy Publications

1. Pre - cious Lord,   take my hand,   Lead me on,   let me
2. When my way   grows drear,   Pre - cious Lord,   lin - ger
3. When the dark - ness ap - pears   And the night   draws

stand,   I   am tired,   I   am weak,   I   am
near,   When my life   is   al - most
near,   And the day   is   past   and

worn.   Through the storm,   through the
gone,   Hear   my   cry,   hear   my
gone,   At   the   riv - er   I

night,   Lead   me   on   to   the   light.   Take   my
call,   Hold   my   hand   lest   I   fall.   Take   my
stand,   Guide   my   feet,   hold   my   hand.   Take   my

hand,   pre - cious Lord,   lead   me   home.
hand,   pre - cious Lord,   lead   me   home.
hand,   pre - cious Lord,   lead   me   home.

Text: Thomas A. Dorsey, 1899–1993
Tune: PRECIOUS LORD, 66 9 D; George N. Allen, 1812–1877; adapt. by Thomas A. Dorsey, 1899–1993; arr. by Kelly Dobbs-Mickus, b.1966
© 1938, (renewed), arr. © 1994, Warner-Tamerlane Publishing Corp.

Verses

me   un - less   the   Fa - ther   beck - ons.
ev - er,_____   you   shall   live   for   ev - er.
blood,   you   shall   not have life with - in   you.
die,_____   you   shall   live   for   ev - er.
come   in - to_____   the_____   world._____

mí   *si mi Pa - dre*   *no lo_a - tra - e.*
siem - pre,_____   *vi - vi - rán*   *por*   *siem - pre.*
san - gre,   *no po -drán* *te - ner* *mi*   *vi - da.*
muer - to,_____   *vi - vi - rán*   *por*   *siem - pre.*
mun - do_____   *pa - ra*   *re - di - mir - nos.*

Refrain

And I will raise   you   up,   and I will
Yo los re - su - ci - ta - ré,   *Yo los re -*

raise   you up,   and I will raise   you
su - ci - ta - ré,   *Yo los re - su - ci - ta -*

up   on the last   day.
ré   *en* *el* *dí - a* *fi - nal.*

Text: John 6 and 11; Suzanne Toolan, RSM, b.1927; tr. anon., rev. by Ronald F. Krisman, b.1946
Tune: BREAD OF LIFE, Irregular with refrain; Suzanne Toolan, RSM, b.1927
© 1966, 1970, 1986, 1993, 2005, GIA Publications, Inc.

114 May the Angels Lead You into Paradise

Cantor, then all:

May the an-gels lead you in-to par-a-dise;

may the mar-tyrs come to wel-come you and

take you to the ho-ly cit-y, the

new and e-ter-nal Je-ru-sa-lem.

Cantor:
May the choir of angels welcome you where Lazarus is poor no longer,
may you have eternal rest, may you have eternal rest.

Text: *In paradisum; Rite of Funerals,* © 1970, ICEL
Tune: Howard Hughes, SM, b.1930, © 1977, ICEL

115 In Paradisum

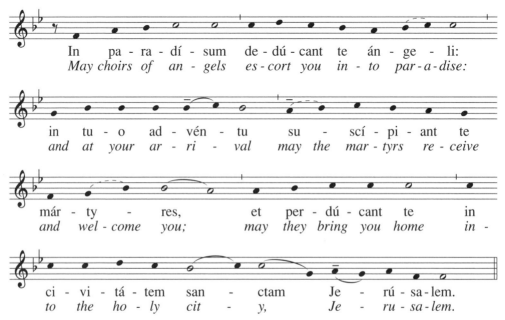

In pa-ra-dí-sum de-dú-cant te án-ge-li:
May choirs of an-gels es-cort you in-to par-a-dise:

in tu-o ad-vén-tu su-scí-pi-ant te
and at your ar-ri-val may the mar-tyrs re-ceive

már-ty-res, et per-dú-cant te in
and wel-come you; may they bring you home in-

ci-vi-tá-tem san-ctam Je-rú-sa-lem.
to the ho-ly cit-y, Je-ru-sa-lem.

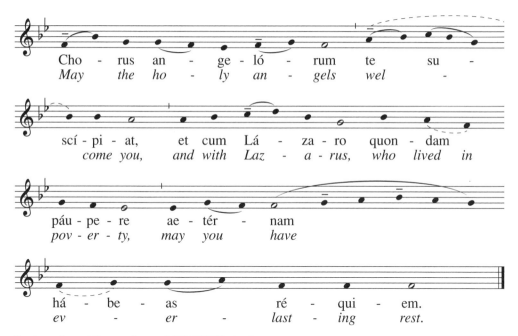

Cho - rus an - ge - ló - rum te su -
May the ho - ly an - gels wel -

scí - pi - at, et cum Lá - za - ro quon - dam
come you, and with Laz - a - rus, who lived in

páu - pe - re ae - tér - nam
pov - er - ty, may you have

há - be - as ré - qui - em.
ev - er - last - ing rest.

Text: *In paradisum* and *Chorus angelorum,* tr. © 1986, GIA Publications, Inc.
Tune: Mode VII; acc. by Richard Proulx, 1937–2010, © 1986, GIA Publications, Inc.

Come, My Way, My Truth, My Life   116

1. Come, my Way, my Truth, my Life: Such a
2. Come, my Light, my Feast, my Strength: Such a
3. Come, my Joy, my Love, my Heart: Such a

way as gives us breath; Such a truth as ends all
light as shows a feast; Such a feast as mends in
joy as none can move; Such a love as none can

strife; Such a life as kill - eth death.
length; Such a strength as makes his guest.
part; Such a heart as joys in love.

Text: George Herbert, 1593–1632
Tune: THE CALL, 7 7 7 7; Ralph Vaughan Williams, 1872–1958

117 Confitémini Dómino / Come and Fill Our Hearts

Ostinato Refrain

Con - fi - té - mi - ni   Dó - mi - no   quó - ni - am
Come and fill our hearts with your peace.   You a - lone, O Lord, are
Spanish: Llé - na - nos, Se - ñor,   de tu paz.   Por - que só - lo e - res
Lithuanian: Aš   pa - si - ti - kiu   Vieš - pa - čiu,   nes   Jis   mums

bo - nus.   Con - fi - té - mi - ni   Dó - mi - no,   Al - le - lú - ia!
ho - ly.   Come and fill our hearts with your peace,   Al - le - lu - ia!
san - to.   Llé - na - nos, Se - ñor,   de tu paz,   ¡A - le - lu - ya!
ge - ras.   Aš   pa - si - ti - kiu   Vieš - pa - čiu,   A - le - liu - ja!

Text: Psalm 136, *Give thanks to the Lord for he is good;* Taizé Community, 1982
Tune: Jacques Berthier, 1923–1994
© 1982, 1991, 2011, Les Presses de Taizé, GIA Publications, Inc., agent

118 Rest Eternal

Refrain

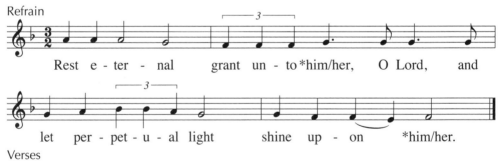

Rest e - ter - nal   grant un - to *him/her,   O Lord,   and

let per - pet - u - al light   shine up - on   *him/her.

Verses

1. It is fitting to sing a hymn to you in Zion:
   all flesh shall come to you.

2. For the souls of the just are in the hands of God:
   no pain shall reach them there.

3. Like a deer that longs for running streams,
   so longs my soul for you.

Or: them

Text: Refrain, Requiem Mass; vs. 1, Psalm 65; vs. 2, Wisdom 3; adapt. by Gail Gillispie, © 2007, World Library Publications;
vs. 3; *Lectionary for Mass,* © 1969, 1981, 1977, ICEL
Music: Gail Gillispie, © 2007, World Library Publications

1. O Lord my God, when I in awe-some
2. When through the woods and for-est glades I
3. And when I think that God, his Son not
4. When Christ shall come with shout of ac-cla-

won-der Con-sid-er all the works thy hands have
wan-der And hear the birds sing sweet-ly in the
spar-ing, Sent him to die, I scarce can take it
ma-tion And take me home, what joy shall fill my

made, I see the stars, I hear the roll-ing
trees, When I look down from loft-y moun-tain
in That on the cross, my bur-den glad-ly
heart! Then I shall bow in hum-ble ad-o-

thun-der, Thy pow'r through-out the u-ni-verse dis-played!
gran-deur And hear the brook and feel the gen-tle breeze,
bear-ing, He bled and died to take a-way my sin!
ra-tion And there pro-claim, "My God, how great thou art!"

Then sings my soul, my Sav-ior God, to thee: How great thou

art, how great thou art! Then sings my soul, my Sav-ior God, to

thee: How great thou art, how great thou art!

Text: Stuart K. Hine, 1899–1989
Tune: HOW GREAT THOU ART, 11 10 11 10 with refrain; Stuart K. Hine, 1899–1989

120　We Walk by Faith

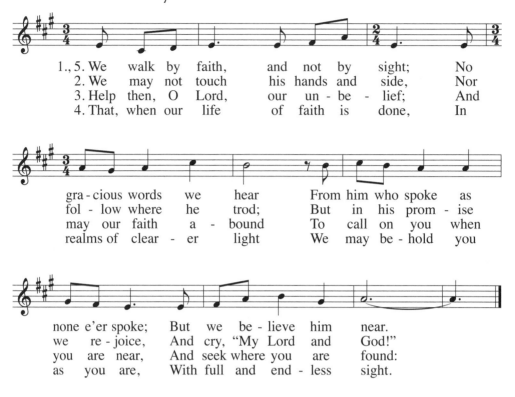

1., 5. We walk by faith, and not by sight; No
2. We may not touch his hands and side, Nor
3. Help then, O Lord, our un - be - lief; And
4. That, when our life of faith is done, In

gra - cious words we hear From him who spoke as
fol - low where he trod; But in his prom - ise
may our faith a - bound To call on you when
realms of clear - er light We may be - hold you

none e'er spoke; But we be - lieve him near.
we re - joice, And cry, "My Lord and God!"
you are near, And seek where you are found:
as you are, With full and end - less sight.

Text: Henry Alford, 1810–1871, alt.
Tune: SHANTI, CM; Marty Haugen, b.1950, © 1984, GIA Publications, Inc.

121　May the Angels Lead You

Cantor, then all:

May the an - gels lead you in - to par - a - dise; may the

mar - tyrs come to wel - come you and take you to the ho - ly

cit - y, the new and e - ter - nal Je - ru - sa - lem.

Cantor:
May the choirs of angels welcome you and lead you to the bosom of Abraham;
and where Lazarus is poor no longer, may you have eternal rest.

Text: *Order of Christian Funerals*, © 1985, ICEL
Music: Steven R. Janco, © 1990, GIA Publications, Inc.

1. I call you to my Fa - ther's
2. Lay down your sor - row, calm your
3. Al - though the way be hard and
4. I have pre - pared a wed - ding
5. I call you to my Fa - ther's

house, A love - ly dwell - ing place.
fear; The Fa - ther bids you come.
long In - to the prom - ised land,
feast Of fin - est food and wine.
house, A love - ly dwell - ing place.

He comes to meet you on the
With o - pen arms he wel - comes
Be not a - fraid to walk with
O join us at this ban - quet
Be not a - fraid to trav - el

road, Arms read - y to em - brace.
you To your e - ter - nal home.
me: I hold you by the hand.
where My friends, the saints, now dine.
there And meet him face to face.

Text: Delores Dufner, OSB, b.1939, © 1983, 2003, GIA Publications, Inc.
Tune: NEW BRITAIN, CM; *Virginia Harmony,* 1831; arr. by Evelyn Simpson-Curenton, b.1953, © 2000, GIA Publications, Inc.

123 O Lord, You Died That All Might Live

1. O Lord, you died that all might live And
2. Lord, bless our friend who died in you. As
3. In green and pleas - ant pas - tures feed The
4. Per - fect us, Lord of pow'r and might, That,

rise to see the per - fect day. The
you have giv - en him/her re - lease, So
sheep that you have sum - moned hence; And
with our friend, we all may come To

full - ness of your mer - cy give To
raise him/her up, your ser - vant true, And
by the still, cool wa - ters lead Your
dwell with - in your cit - y bright, Je -

this our friend for whom we pray.
give him/her ev - er - last - ing peace.
flock in lov - ing prov - i - dence.
ru - sa - lem, our heav'n - ly home.

O Lamb of God, Re - deem - er blest, Grant

him/her e - ter - nal light and rest.

Text: Richard F. Littledale, 1833–1890, alt.
Tune: MELITA, LM with refrain; John B. Dykes, 1823–1876

1. Rest in peace, earth's jour - ney end - ed, You whom Christ re -
2. Hap - py soul, to Christ u - nit - ed, Calm - er now and
3. May we meet, dear Lord, in heav - en, Each for - giv - ing,

deemed, de - fend - ed: To the place where saints are one,
clear - er - sight - ed: Your new jour - ney now be - gins,
each for - giv - en, Each more gift - ed to pur - sue

Safe - ly brought by him a - lone. May he grant us
Freed from earth's be - set - ting sins. Press - ing on - ward
All you have for us to do. By your Spir - it's

like pro - tec - tion. Rest in peace, rest in peace,
to per - fec - tion, Hap - py soul, hap - py soul,
sure di - rec - tion May we meet, may we meet,

Rest in peace, earth's jour - ney end - ed.
Hap - py soul, to Christ u - nit - ed.
May we meet, dear Lord, in heav - en.

Text: Fred Pratt Green, 1903–2000, © 1982, Hope Publishing Company
Music: MOEHR, 88 77 8 6 8; Russell Schulz-Widmar, b.1944, © 1987, GIA Publications, Inc.

125 Nada Te Turbe / Nothing Can Trouble

Ostinato Refrain

Na - da te tur - be, na - da te es-pan - te. Quien a Dios tie - ne
Noth-ing can trou-ble, noth-ing can fright-en. Those who seek God shall
*Korean:두 려 워 말 라 걱 정 을 말 라 주 님 계 시 니

na - da le fal - ta. So - lo Dios bas - ta.
nev-er go want - ing. God a - lone fills us.
아 쉬 움 없 네 주 님 안 에 서

Korean transliteration: Du-lyeo-wo mal-la geog-jeong-eul mal-la
Ju-nim gye-si-ni a-swi-um eobs-ne.
Du-lyeo-wo mal-la geog-jeong-eul mal-la
Ju-nim an-e-seo.

Text: St. Teresa of Jesus; Taizé Community, 1986, 1991
Tune: Jacques Berthier, 1923–1994
© 1986, 1991, Les Presses de Taizé, GIA Publications, Inc., agent

126 For All the Saints Who've Shown Your Love

1. For all the saints who've shown your love In how they
2. For all the saints who loved your name, Whose faith in -
3. For all the saints who named your will, And showed the
4. Bless all whose will or name or love Re - flects the

live and where they move, For mind - ful wom - en,
creased the Sav - ior's fame, Who sang your songs and
king - dom com - ing still Through self - less pro - test,
grace of heav'n a - bove. Though un - ac - claimed by

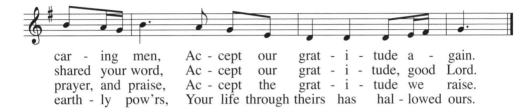

car - ing men, Ac - cept our grat - i - tude a - gain.
shared your word, Ac - cept our grat - i - tude, good Lord.
prayer, and praise, Ac - cept the grat - i - tude we raise.
earth - ly pow'rs, Your life through theirs has hal - lowed ours.

Text: John L. Bell, b.1949, © 1996, Iona Community, GIA Publications, Inc., agent
Tune: O WALY WALY, LM; English melody; arr. by John L. Bell, b.1949, © 1989, Iona Community, GIA Publications, Inc., agent

Dwellers in the Holy City   127

1. Dwell - ers in the ho - ly cit - y,
2. Fam - 'ly born to God's own house - hold,
3. Sing - ers in the choir of heav - en,
4. Saints a - round the ban - quet gath - ered,

O - pen wide the gold - en door; May our
Bring our faith - ful friend with - in, Free of
Let your prayer like in - cense rise; Let our
Claim her/him now as next of kin; Lead her/him

friend from this world sum - moned Know God's pres - ence
suf - f'ring, pain and sor - row, Free of weak - ness,
friend, in song, now join you, Prais - ing God in
to the fam - 'ly ta - ble; Let the feast of

ev - er - more. Saints and an - gels, make her/him
free of sin. May her/his pass - ing lead to
par - a - dise. And may we, re - joic - ing,
joy be - gin. Friends at God's own ta - ble

wel - come, Glad at home for ev - er - more.
glo - ry, Vic - t'ry o - ver death and sin.
join you, Prais - ers all in par - a - dise.
seat - ed, Let the feast - ing now be - gin!

Text: Delores Dufner, OSB, b.1939, © 2011, GIA Publications, Inc.
Tune: LAUDA ANIMA, 8 7 8 7 8 7; John Goss, 1800–1880

128   Unless a Grain of Wheat

Refrain

Un - less   a   grain   of   wheat   shall   fall   up -
on   the   ground   and   die,   it   re - mains   but   a
sin - gle   grain   with   no   life.

Verses

1. If   we   have   died   with   him,   then   we   shall
2. If   an - y - one   serves   me,   then   they   must
3. Make   your   home   in   me   as   I   make
4. If   you   re - main   in   me   and   my   word
5. Those   who   love   me   are   loved   by   my
6. Peace   I   leave   with   you,   my   peace   I

live   with   him;   if   we   hold   firm,   we   shall
fol - low   me;   where - ev - er   I   am,   my
mine   in   you;   those   who   re - main   in   me
lives   in   you,   then   you   will   be   my   dis -
Fa - ther;   we   shall   be   with   them   and
give   to   you;   peace   which   the   world   can - not

D.C.

reign   with   him.
ser - vants   will   be.
bear   much   fruit.
ci - ples.
dwell   in   them.
give   is   my   gift.

Text: John 12:24; Bernadette Farrell, b.1957
Tune: Bernadette Farrell, b.1957
© 1983, Bernadette Farrell. Published by OCP.

1. There is a place pre-pared for lit-tle
2. There is a place where hands which held ours
3. There is a place where all the lost po-
4. There is a place where God will hear our
5. Je-sus, who bids us be like lit-tle

chil-dren, Those we once lived for, those we deep-ly
tight-ly Now are re-leased be-yond all hurt and
ten-tial Yields its full prom-ise, finds its true in-
ques-tions, Suf-fer our an-ger, share our speech-less
chil-dren, Shields those our arms are yearn-ing to em-

mourn, Those who from play, from learn-ing and from
fear, Healed by that love which al-so feels our
tent; Si-lenced no more, young voic-es ech-o
grief, Gen-tly re-pair the in-no-cence of
brace. God will en-sure that all are re-u-

laugh-ter, Cruel-ly were torn.
sor-row Tear af-ter tear.
free-ly As they were meant.
lov-ing And of be-lief.
nit-ed; There is a place.

Text: John L. Bell, b.1949
Tune: DUNBLANE PRIMARY, 11 10 11 4; John L. Bell, b.1949
© 1996, Iona Community, GIA Publications, Inc., agent

130 Stainless the Maiden / Serdeczna Matko

1. Stain - less the Maid - en whom he chose for moth - er;
2. Lan - tern in dark - ness, when the sick are sigh - ing,
3. Je - sus has con - quered; to his side he raised her;
1. Ser - de - czna Ma - tko, O - pie - kun - ko lu - dzi,
2. Do ko - góż ma - my, wzdy - chać nę - dzne dzia - tki?
3. Za - słu - ży - li - śmy, to praw - da, przez zło - ści,

Nine months she wait - ed, bear - ing Christ, our broth - er;
Thresh - old of bright - ness, com - fort for the dy - ing,
Queen of the an - gels, ev - 'ry saint has praised her.
Niech Cię płacz sie - rot do li - to - ści wzbu - dzi!
Tyl - ko do Cie - bie, u - ko - cha - nej Ma - tki:
By nas Bóg ka - rał ró - zgą su - ro - wo - ści

Think of her glad - ness when at last she saw him:
High she is hold - ing for a world a - dor - ing,
Yet, in her splen - dor, Mar - y goes on draw - ing
Wy - gnań - cy E - wy, do Cie - bie wo - ła - my:
U któ - rej Ser - ce o - twar - te ka - żde - mu,
Lecz kie - dy Oj - ciec ro - zgnie - wa - ny sie - cze,

Repeat ad lib.

God in a man - ger, Beth - le - hem a heav - en!
Hope of the na - tions, Je - sus Christ, our broth - er.
Sin - ners and ex - iles to their prom - ised glo - ry.
Zli - tuj się, zli - tuj, niech się nie tu - ła - my!
A o - so - bli - wie nę - dzą stra - pio - ne - mu!
Szczę - śli - wy kto się do Ma - tki u - cie - cze.

Text: Polish traditional; English paraphrase by Willard F. Jabusch, b.1930, © 1976, 1977
Tune: SERDECZNA MATKO, 11 11 D; Polish traditional; adapt. by Kelly Dobbs-Mickus, b.1966, from an arr. by Richard Proulx, 1937–2010,
    © 2011, GIA Publications, Inc.

Come to Me 131

Refrain

Come to me, come to me, come when you are wea-ry;
come to me, come to me, and I will give you rest.

Verses 1, 2

1. All who la-bor and are bur-dened,
2. Take my yoke up-on your shoul-ders,

all who la-bor and are bur-dened, let them come to me,
take my yoke up-on your shoul-ders, come and learn from me,

D.C.

come to me, and I will give them rest.
learn from me, for I am gen-tle of heart.

Verse 3

3. For the heart I hold is hum-ble, yes, the

heart I hold is hum-ble, and my yoke is eas-y, my

D.C.

bur-den light, and you will find rest for your souls.

Text: Matthew 11:28–30; Michael Joncas, b.1951
Tune: Michael Joncas, b.1951

132 Make Me a Channel of Your Peace

Verses 1, 2, 4

1. Make me a chan-nel of your peace. Where
2. Make me a chan-nel of your peace. Where
4. Make me a chan-nel of your peace. It

there is ha-tred, let me bring your love. Where
there's de-spair in life, let me bring hope. Where
is in par-don-ing that we are par-doned, in

there is in-ju-ry, your par-don, Lord, And
there is dark-ness, on-ly light, And
giv-ing of our-selves that we re-ceive, and in

where there's doubt, true faith in you.
where there's sad-ness, ev-er joy.
dy-ing that we're born to e-ter-nal life.

Verse 3

3. Oh, Mas-ter, grant that I may nev-er seek So much to be con-

soled as to con-sole. To be un-der-stood as to un-der-

D.C.

stand. To be loved as to love with all my soul.

Text: Prayer of St. Francis; adapt. by Sebastian Temple, 1928–1997
Tune: Sebastian Temple, 1928–1997; acc. by Robert J. Batastini, b.1942
© 1967, OCP
Dedicated to Mrs. Frances Tracy

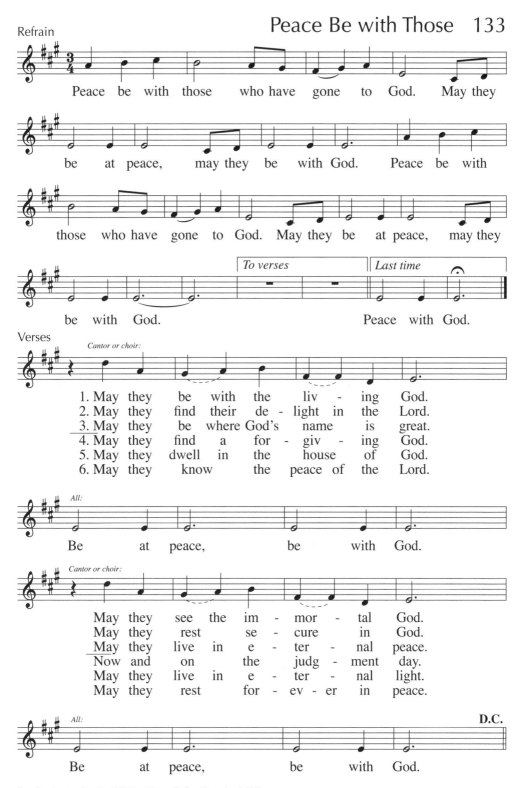

Text: Based on text from the 1969 *Rite of Funerals*; Carol Browning, b.1956
Tune: Carol Browning, b.1956
© 2008, GIA Publications, Inc.

134 Only You, O God

Refrain

On - ly you, O God, and you a-lone, the
bro - ken heart con - sole, On-ly you, O God, and
you a-lone, the wound - ed world make whole.

Verses

1. O God, our rock and ha - ven, Our
2. You guard us, faith - ful fa - ther, With-
3. We pray do not a - ban - don The

strong - hold, safe and sure, Though earth be torn and
in your shel - t'ring palm; You nurse us, lov - ing
ones you call your own; Our com - fort and com -

D.C.

shak - en, In you we stand se - cure.
moth - er, With milk and heal - ing balm.
pan - ion, We trust in you a - lone.

Text: Susan R. Briehl, b.1952, © 2003, GIA Publications, Inc.
Tune: BALM IN GILEAD, 7 6 7 6 with refrain; African American spiritual; acc. by Marty Haugen, b.1950, © 2003, GIA Publications, Inc.

Quietly, Peacefully 135

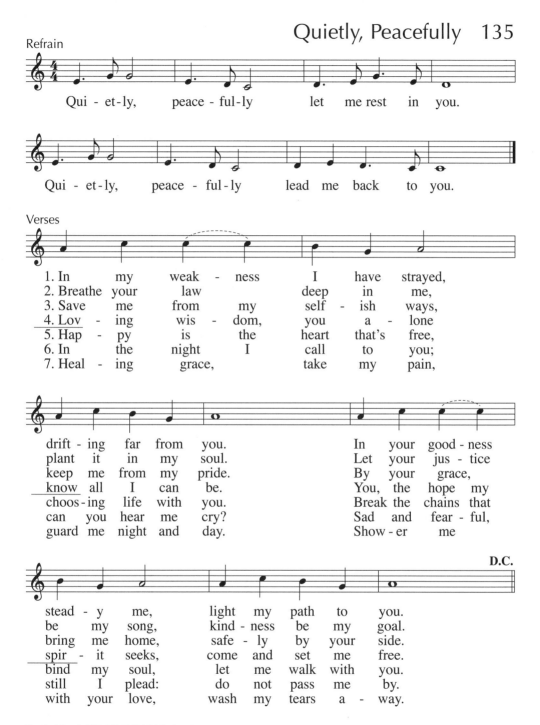

Refrain

Qui - et-ly, peace - ful-ly let me rest in you.

Qui - et-ly, peace - ful-ly lead me back to you.

Verses

1. In my weak - ness I have strayed,
2. Breathe your law deep in me,
3. Save me from my self - ish ways,
4. Lov - ing wis - dom, you a - lone
5. Hap - py is the heart that's free,
6. In the night I call to you;
7. Heal - ing grace, take my pain,

drift - ing far from you. In your good - ness
plant it in my soul. Let your jus - tice
keep me from my pride. By your grace,
know all I can be. You, the hope my
choos - ing life with you. Break the chains that
can you hear me cry? Sad and fear - ful,
guard me night and day. Show - er me

D.C.

stead - y me, light my path to you.
be my song, kind - ness be my goal.
bring me home, safe - ly by your side.
spir - it seeks, come and set me free.
bind my soul, let me walk with you.
still I plead: do not pass me by.
with your love, wash my tears a - way.

Text: Lori True, b.1961, © 2007, GIA Publications, Inc.
Tune: Antonin Dvořák, 1841–1904; adapt. by Lori True, b.1961, © 2007, GIA Publications, Inc.

136 Resucitó

Refrain

Re - su - ci - tó, re - su - ci - tó, re - su - ci -
A - le - lu - ya, a - le - lu - ya, a - le - lu -

To verses | *Final ending*

tó, a - le - lu - ya. A - le - lu - ya.
ya, re - su - ci - tó.

Verses

1. La muer - te ¿dón - de es - tá la
2. Gra - cias se - an da - das al
3. A - le - grí - a, a - le - grí - a her -
4. Si con Él mo - ri - mos, y con Él vi -

1. And death now, van - ished is the
2. The king - dom, praise to God, the
3. Our glad - ness, bliss - ful in our
4. With him then, die and live with

muer - te? ¿Dón - de es - tá mi
Pa - dre que nos pa - só a su
ma - nos, que si hoy nos que -
vi - mos, y con Él can -

fear now, ban - ished are my
king - dom! Raised up to the
glad - ness, this will be our
him then, rise and sing our

D.C.

muer - te? ¿Dón - de su vic - to - ria?
rei - no dón - de se vi - ve de a - mor.
re - mos es que re - su - ci - tó.
ta - mos. y ¡A - le - lu - ya!

tears now, death has passed a - way.
king - dom, we shall live in love.
glad - ness, that he is a - live.
hymn then, sing al - le - lu - ia.

Text: Kiko Argüello, © 1972, Ediciones Musical PAX, U.S. agent: OCP; tr. © 1988, OCP
Tune: Kiko Argüello, © 1972, Ediciones Musical PAX, U.S. agent: OCP; acc. by Diana Kodner, b.1957

Shelter Me, O God   137

Refrain

Shel-ter me, O God; hide me in the shad-ow of your wings. You a-lone are my hope.

Verses

1. When my foes sur-round me, set me high a-bove their
2. As a moth - er gath - ers her young be-neath her
3. Though I walk in dark-ness, through the nee - dle's eye of

D.C.

reach. Hear me when I call your name.
care, gath - er me in - to your arms.
death, you will nev - er leave my side.

Text: Psalm 16:1, 61:5, Luke 13:34; Bob Hurd, b.1950, © 1984, Bob Hurd
Tune: Bob Hurd, b.1950, © 1984, Bob Hurd; harm. by Craig S. Kingsbury, b.1952, © 1984, OCP
Published by OCP.

Steal Away to Jesus   138

Refrain

Steal a-way, steal a-way, steal a-way to Je-sus!

Steal a-way, steal a-way home, I ain't got long to stay here.

Verses

1. My Lord, he calls me, He calls me by the thun - der; The
2. Green trees are bend-ing, Poor sin - ners stand a trem-bling; The
3. My Lord, he calls me, He calls me by the light-ning; The

D.C.

trum-pet sounds with - in my soul; I ain't got long to stay here.

Text: African American spiritual
Tune: African American spiritual

139 You Are Near

Refrain

O Lord, I know you are near, stand-ing al-ways at my side. You guard me from the foe, and you lead me in ways ev-er-last-ing.

Verses

1. Lord, you have searched my heart, and you
2. Where can I run from your love? If I
3. You know my heart and its ways, you who
4. Mar-vel-ous to me are your works; how pro -

know when I sit and when I stand. Your
climb to the heav-ens you are there; if I
formed me be-fore I was born, in the
found are your thoughts, my Lord. E-ven

hand is up-on me, pro-tect-ing me from death,
fly to the sun-rise or sail be-yond the sea,
se-cret of dark-ness be-fore I saw the sun,
if I could count them, they num-ber as the stars,

keep-ing me from harm.
still I'd find you there.
in my moth-er's womb.
you would still be there.

Text: Psalm 139; Dan Schutte, b.1947
Tune: Dan Schutte, b.1947; acc. by Sr. Theophane Hytrek, OSF, 1915–1992
© 1971, 2008, OCP

Refrain

The hand of God shall hold you, the peace of God en-fold you, the love that dreamed and formed you still sur-rounds you here to-day; The light of God be-side you, a-bove, be-neath, in-side you, the light that shines to guide you home to the lov-ing hand of God.

Verses

1. May God's light shine ever upon you, may you rest in the arms of God;
   may you dwell for evermore in communion with all the blessed.

2. May the angels lead you into paradise; may the martyrs come to welcome you
   and take you to the holy city, the new and eternal Jerusalem.

141 We Shall Rise Again

1. Come to me, all you wea - ry,
2. Though we walk through the dark - ness,
3. We de - pend on God's mer - cy,
4. Do not fear death's do - min - ion,
5. At the door there to greet us,

with your bur - dens and pain.
e - vil we do not fear.
mer - cy which nev - er fades.
look be - yond earth and grave.
mar - tyrs, an - gels, and saints,

Take my yoke on your shoul - ders and
You are walk - ing be - side us with your
We re - mem - ber our cov - e - nant and the
See the bright - ness of Je - sus shin - ing
And our fam - 'ly and loved ones, ev - 'ry -

learn from me: I am gen - tle and
rod and your staff. On - ly good - ness and
prom - ise Je - sus made: If we die with Christ
out to light our way. Lov - ing Fa - ther and
one freed from their chains. We shall feel their ac -

hum - ble, and your soul will find rest,
kind - ness fol - low us all our lives.
Je - sus, we shall live with him,
Spir - it, lov - ing Je - sus the Son,
cep - tance, and the joy of new life.

For my yoke is eas - y and my
We shall dwell in the Lord's house for so
And if we are faith - ful, we shall
All God's peo - ple to - geth - er, we shall
We shall join in the gath - er - ing, re - u -

bur - den is light.
man - y years to come!
reign with him!
live on as one!
nit - ed in God's love!

We shall rise a - gain on the last day with the

faith - ful, rich and poor. Com-ing to the house of Lord

Je - sus, we will find an o - pen door there, we will

find an o - pen door.

Text: Matthew 11:29–30, Psalm 23, John 11, 2 Timothy 2; Jeremy Young, b.1948
Tune: RESURRECTION; Irregular with refrain; Jeremy Young, b.1948
© 1987, GIA Publications, Inc.

142 Lord of the Living

1. Lord of the liv - ing, in your name as - sem - bled,
2. Help us to treas - ure all that will re - mind us
3. May we, when - ev - er tempt - ed to de - jec - tion
4. God, you can lift us from the grave of sor - row

We join to thank you for the life re -
Of the en - rich - ment in the days be -
Strong - ly re - cap - ture thoughts of res - ur -
In - to the pres - ence of your own to -

mem - bered. Hold us, en - fold us, to your chil - dren
hind us. Your love has set us in the gen - er -
rec - tion. You gave us Je - sus to de - feat our
mor - row; Give to your peo - ple for the day's af -

giv - ing Hope in be - liev - ing.
a - tions, God of cre - a - tion.
sad - ness With Eas - ter glad - ness.
flic - tion Your ben - e - dic - tion.

Text: Fred Kaan, 1929–2009, © 1968, Hope Publishing Company
Tune: CHRISTE SANCTORUM, 11 11 11 5; Paris *Antiphoner*, 1681

1. E - ter - nal Fa - ther, strong to save, Whose arm has bound the
2. O Sav - ior, whose al - might - y word The wind and waves sub -
3. O Ho - ly Spir - it, who did brood Up - on the cha - os
4. O Trin - i - ty of love and pow'r, All trav - 'lers guard in

rest - less wave, Who bade the might - y o - cean deep Its
mis - sive heard, Who walked up - on the foam - ing deep, And
wild and rude, And bade its an - gry tu - mult cease, And
dan - ger's hour; From rock and tem - pest, fire and foe, Pro -

own ap - point - ed lim - its keep: O hear us when we
calm a - mid its rage did sleep: O hear us when we
gave, for fierce con - fu - sion, peace: O hear us when we
tect them where - so - e'er they go; Thus ev - er - more shall

cry to thee For those in per - il on the sea.
cry to thee For those in per - il on the sea.
cry to thee For those in per - il on the sea.
rise to thee Glad praise from air and land and sea.

Text: William Whiting, 1825–1878
Tune: MELITA, 88 88 88; John Bacchus Dykes, 1823–1876

144 Be Still, My Soul

1. Be still, my soul: the Lord is on your side.
2. Be still, my soul: your God will un - der - take
3. Be still, my soul: the hour is has - t'ning on

Bear pa - tient - ly the cross of grief or pain;
To guide the fu - ture, as in a - ges past.
When we shall be for ev - er with the Lord,

Leave to your God to or - der and pro - vide;
Your hope, your con - fi - dence let noth - ing shake;
When dis - ap - point - ment, grief, and fear are gone,

In ev - 'ry change God faith - ful will re - main.
All now mys - te - rious shall be bright at last.
Sor - row for - got, love's pur - est joys re - stored.

Be still, my soul: your best, your heav'n - ly friend
Be still, my soul: the waves and winds still know
Be still, my soul: when change and tears are past,

Through thorn - y ways leads to a joy - ful end.
The Christ who ruled them while he dwelt be - low.
All safe and bless - ed we shall meet at last.

Text: Katharina von Schlegel, 1697–1768; tr. by Jane L. Borthwick, 1813–1897. alt.
Tune: FINLANDIA, 10 10 10 10 10 10; Jean Sibelius, 1865–1957

May ho - ly an - gels lead you forth to par - a - dise,

and may the mar - tyrs greet your com - ing home.

May you find wel - come there with - in God's dwell-ing - place,

the rad - iant cit - y, New Je - ru - sa - lem.

May an - gel choirs re - ceive you, sing - ing joy - ful - ly,

as you be - hold with La - za - rus, once poor,

the bless-ed vi - sion of the Ho - ly Trin - i - ty.

May you know rest and peace with God for - ev - er - more.

Text: *In paradisum* and *Chorus angelorum*; Latin 11th C.; para. by Ronald F. Krisman, b.1946, © 2011, GIA Publications, Inc.
Tune: LONDONDERRY AIRE, 11 10 11 10 D; arr. by John L. Bell, b.1949, © 1996, Iona Community, GIA Publications, Inc., agent

146 Song of Farewell

Refrain

Dy-ing you de-stroyed our death! Ris-ing you re - stored our life!

Lord Je - sus, Lord Je - sus, come in glo - ry!

Verses

1. May Christ who died for you lead you into his kingdom;
   may Christ who died for you lead you this day into paradise.

2. May Christ, the Good Shepherd, lead you home today
   and give you a place within his flock.

Alternate children's verse:
2. May Christ, the Good Shepherd, take you on his shoulders
   and bring you home, bring you home today.

3. May the angels lead you into paradise;
   may the martyrs come to welcome you
   and take you to the Holy City, the new and eternal Jerusalem.

4. May the choirs of angels come to meet you,
   may the choirs of angels come to meet you;
   where Lazarus is poor no longer, may you have eternal life in Christ.

Alternate children's verse:
4. May the choirs of angels come to meet you,
   may the choirs of angels come to meet you;
   and with all God's children may you have eternal life in Christ.

Text: Memorial Acclamation, © 1973, ICEL; *In paradisum;* Michael Marchal, b.1951, © 1988, GIA Publications, Inc.
Tune: Michael Joncas, b.1951, © 1988, GIA Publications, Inc.

Refrain

May the choirs of an - gels come to greet you. May they

speed you to par - a - dise. May the Lord en - fold you

To verses | *Last time*

in his mer - cy. May you find e - ter - nal life. life.

Verses

1. The Lord is my light and my help; it is
2. There is one thing I ask of the Lord; that he
3. O Lord, hear my voice when I cry; have
4. I am sure I shall see the Lord's good-ness; I shall

he who pro - tects me from harm. The
grant me my heart - felt de - sire. To
mer - cy on me and give an - swer. Do not
dwell in the land of the liv - ing. Hope in

Lord is the strength of my days; be - fore
dwell in the courts of our God ev - 'ry
cast me a - way in your an - ger, for
God, stand firm and take heart,

D.C.

whom should I trem - ble with fear?
day of my life in his pres - ence.
you are the God of my help.
place all your trust in the Lord.

Text: *In paradisum* and Psalm 27; Ernest Sands, b.1949
Tune: Ernest Sands, b.1949
© 1990, Ernest Sands. Published by OCP.

148 Hail Mary: Gentle Woman

Hail Mar - y, full of grace, the
Lord is with you. Bless-ed are you a - mong
wom-en, and blest is the fruit of your womb, Je - sus.
Ho-ly Mar - y, Moth-er of God,
pray for us sin - ners now and at the hour of
death. A - men.

℣ Refrain

Gen-tle wom-an, qui-et light, morn-ing
star, so strong and bright, gen-tle
Moth-er, peace-ful dove, teach us
wis - dom; teach us love.

Verse 1

1. You were cho - sen by the Fa - ther;

you were cho - sen for the Son.

You were cho - sen from all wom-en

D.S.

and for wom-an, shin-ing one.

Verse 2

2. Bless-ed are you a - mong wom-en,

blest in turn all wom-en, too.

Bless-ed they with peace - ful spir-its.

D.S.

Bless-ed they with gen - tle hearts.

Text: *Hail Mary*, alt.; Carey Landry, b.1944
Tune: Carey Landry, b.1944; arr. by Martha Lesinski, alt.
© 1975, 1978, Carey Landry and North American Liturgy Resources. Published by OCP.

Vigil for the Deceased

149

Following the death of a Christian, the Church provides a number of rites to honor the deceased and comfort the mourners. The Vigil for the Deceased, commonly known as a wake service, may take place in a funeral home, the church, or even in the home of the deceased. The vigil provides an opportunity for the gathered community and family to share remembrances about the deceased, to pray for the deceased, and to pray for and comfort one another.

INTRODUCTORY RITES

GREETING
All present are greeted by the leader and respond: **And with your spirit.**

OPENING SONG
An opening song may be sung.

INVITATION TO PRAYER
All are invited to pray silently.

OPENING PRAYER
At the conclusion of the prayer, all respond: **Amen.**

LITURGY OF THE WORD

FIRST READING
A reading from Scripture is proclaimed.

RESPONSORIAL PSALM
A psalm (nos. 26–46) may be sung.

GOSPEL
A reading from one of the gospels is proclaimed.

HOMILY OR REFLECTION
A priest or deacon may offer a brief homily; a parish staff member or acquaintance of the deceased may offer a brief reflection on the readings.

PRAYER OF INTERCESSION

LITANY
All respond: **Lord, have mercy.**

THE LORD'S PRAYER

Assembly: **Our Father, who art in heaven,**
hallowed be thy name;
thy kingdom come,
thy will be done on earth as it is in heaven.
Give us this day our daily bread,
and forgive us our trespasses,
as we forgive those who trespass against us;
and lead us not into temptation,
but deliver us from evil.

CONCLUDING PRAYER

At the conclusion of the prayer, all respond: **Amen.** *A member or a friend of the family may speak in remembrance of the deceased.*

CONCLUDING RITES

BLESSING

The leader prays a short prayer and then says:

Leader: Eternal rest grant unto him/her, Lord.

Assembly: **And let perpetual light shine upon him/her.**

Leader: May his/her soul and the souls of all the faithful departed,
through the mercy of God, rest in peace.

Assembly: **Amen.**

A final prayer is prayed and at its conclusion all respond: **Amen.**

Rite of Committal

The Rite of Committal is normally celebrated at the site of the grave in the cemetery. It is the last of the Church's funeral rites for the deceased. Family and friends gather to take the deceased to his or her final resting place. The celebration also honors the place of interment, where family and friends will continue to visit and remember the deceased.

As the family and friends gather, a song may be sung.

INVITATION
All are invited to pray.

SCRIPTURE
A brief Scripture passage is read.

PRAYER OVER THE PLACE OF COMMITAL
At the conclusion of the prayer, all respond: **Amen.**

COMMITTAL
The body or cremated remains is placed in its final resting place.

INTERCESSIONS
All respond: **Lord, have mercy.**

THE LORD'S PRAYER
Assembly: **Our Father, who art in heaven,**
hallowed be thy name;
thy kingdom come,
thy will be done on earth as it is in heaven.
Give us this day our daily bread,
and forgive us our trespasses,
as we forgive those who trespass against us;
and lead us not into temptation,
but deliver us from evil.

PRAYER OVER THE PEOPLE
At the conclusion of the prayer, all respond: **Amen.**

The leader then says the following:
Leader: Eternal rest grant unto him/her, Lord.
Assembly: **And let perpetual light shine upon him/her.**
Leader: May his/her soul and the souls of all the faithful departed,
through the mercy of God, rest in peace.
Assembly: **Amen.**

A final prayer is prayed and at its conclusion all respond: **Amen.**

The service concludes:
Leader: Go in the peace of Christ.
Assembly: **Thanks be to God.**

If customary, flowers or soil may be placed be placed on the coffin. A song may be sung at this time.

Acknowledgments/*continued*

Index of First Lines and Common Titles/*continued*

ISBN: 978-1-62277-003-8